HAUNTED
FLORIDA
LIGHTHOUSES

HAUNTED
FLORIDA
LIGHTHOUSES

HEATHER LEIGH, PhD

Haunted
America

Published by Haunted America
A Division of The History Press
Charleston, SC
www.historypress.com

First published 2023

Manufactured in the United States

ISBN 9781467153836

Library of Congress Control Number: 2023937161

Notice: The information in this book is true and complete to the best of our knowledge. It is offered without guarantee on the part of the author or The History Press. The author and The History Press disclaim all liability in connection with the use of this book.

I want to dedicate this book to my family, who continue to put up with my crazy paranormal adventures. I love you, Josh, Aidan, Papa, Mama and Liam.

I also want to dedicate this book to Christopher Brito (1973–1995), a special person in my life and someone I continue to think of and miss dearly. Thank you for visiting me now and then in my dreams. Until we meet again, Christopher!

CONTENTS

CONTENTS

FOREWORD

As chief investigative officer for the Warren Legacy Foundation and someone who has devoted the last thirty-seven years of his life to researching paranormal phenomena, I have come to the reasonable conclusion that, in my humble opinion, ghosts indeed do exist. As far back as I can remember, I have always had a deep fascination with the occult and the allure of the unknown. I have always possessed a skeptical yet insatiable interest in the existence of ghosts, demons, poltergeists and other strange phenomena that seemingly offer no natural or scientific explanation. And although I acknowledge that paranormal research can be a very divisive and controversial topic, it is one that I have found worthy of close exploration. To that end, I have vowed to dedicate my life to researching the unusual and the unexplained. To help others face their fears, understand and overcome their paranormal afflictions. And to help educate those who will follow. It is my destiny: my divine vocation.

My journey into the paranormal realm began in September 1986 when I attended a lecture hosted by world-renowned psychic researchers Ed and Lorraine Warren at a local hotel. I remember meeting Lorraine for the first time as I approached the registration table and exchanged salutations. With a sweet smile and a bewildered look, Lorraine cocked her head to one side and asked if we had ever met. Of course, we had not. She said she sensed a reason for me coming there that night and asked if we could speak privately after the presentation. I remember being so excited that I could hardly keep a thought in my head. When the program concluded, Lorraine invited me to join her and Ed at the diner across the street. We sat across from one another as she held my hand and began reading my aura. She said, "Honey, you were born to do this work," and asked if I would like to come and work with them—an invitation I eagerly accepted.

I then spent the next thirty-three years working and studying under the tutelage of Ed and Lorraine until their passing in 2006 and 2019, respectively. They took me under their wing and treated me like one of their own: like family. As Lorraine always told me, I was their adopted grandson. They introduced me to their work and shared all their knowledge and expertise. They were lovely people, caring mentors and even better friends. After Lorraine passed, I promised to continue their work—work that I so deeply love and enjoy. I am proud to carry on their legacy.

Dr. Heather Leigh is a good personal friend and learned colleague whom I have known for some time. As a lighthouse enthusiast, I was deeply honored and excited when Heather asked me to write the foreword to her new book, *Haunted Florida Lighthouses*. The book further showcases Heather's literary talents as she uncovers the mysterious and storied history of some of the most iconic beacons dotting the coasts of Florida. The integrity of Dr. Heather Leigh's work as an author, lecturer, educator, and paranormal investigator is well known and respected throughout the paranormal world. Her superb, unsurpassed attention to facts and detail is a testament to her meticulous research and tireless work ethic. I sincerely hope you will enjoy and appreciate her work as much as I have. I promise you will not be disappointed.

Joe Franke

ACKNOWLEDGEMENTS

My family, Josh and Aidan, have been a significant part of my paranormal endeavors. I am so happy to have them by my side when investigating and exploring haunted locations.

I want to thank Joe Franke for the remarkable foreword and all of his guidance as we adventure through the world of the paranormal together.

To my co-host of Ghost Education 101, I want to thank Philip R. Wyatt for the fantastic photos and evidence he shared with me from his investigation at the St. Augustine Lighthouse.

INTRODUCTION

Lighthouses are endlessly suggestive signifiers of both human isolation and our ultimate connectedness to each other.
—Virginia Woolf

Oddly enough, lighthouses have been a significant part of American history, many easily identified by a simple picture. These magnificent structures located on coastlines not only served a purpose for ships at sea looking for local ports and avoiding dangerous shorelines and hidden reefs, but they also served as a primary residence for lighthouse keepers and their families.

Operating a lighthouse was a way of life. Lighthouse keepers and their families lived on the property, working, playing, laughing and growing up with a way of life like no other in the country. In many situations, being a lighthouse keeper was a lonely job, and it could be weeks or months before keepers or their families had any interaction with other humans. Unfortunately, many keepers' and families' attachments to these properties fueled the paranormal reports associated with lighthouses.

Today, paranormal researchers are amazed by how much activity and data they can collect at a lighthouse. There is so much activity on the stairs of the lighthouse, on the property, near the shoreline and in the keeper's residence. So it is no wonder why paranormal activity is attracted to the many lighthouses nationwide.

The Cape Florida
Lighthouse in Key
Biscayne, a barrier
island town across
the Rickenbacker
Causeway from
Miami, Florida.
*Library of Congress,
Carol M. Highsmith.*

Surrounded by water on all three sides, Florida is home to many lighthouses, and most of those lighthouses are considered some of the most haunted locations in Florida.

Lighthouses in Florida represent a simpler life, but each one has a spooky history, confirmed by the many paranormal claims from owners, visitors and researchers. Unfortunately, many lighthouses have a dreadful past, including murdered lighthouse keepers, troubled children, restless soldiers and pirates, fueling the rumors that these magnificent locations have become haunted.

Lighthouses act as beacons of light and safety, which could be why so many spirits and other entities are attracted to these locations—especially for those sailors, captains and passengers who may have died from pirate attacks or coastal accidents when these beacons were inoperable or long before they were constructed.

The earliest known lighthouses are some of the many wonders of the ancient world, including the Pharos of Alexandria, believed to have been built sometime before 270 BC. This lighthouse lit the Mediterranean Sea for almost a millennium and inspired the Roman Empire to make around thirty more lighthouses around the Mediterranean and the Atlantic coast of Europe.

Unfortunately, lighthouses disappeared from architectural records until the later Middle Ages and early days of the Renaissance. The next lighthouse on record is the Meloria Lighthouse, built in 1157 to light the coast of Tuscany. Shortly after, other coastal countries, such as Spain, Portugal, France and England, began their plans to construct lighthouses.[1]

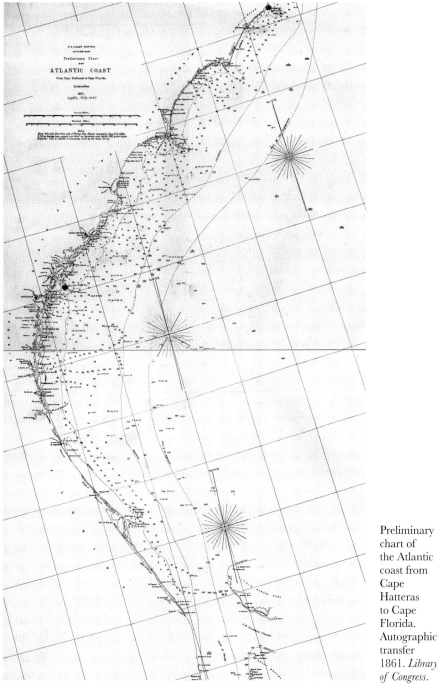

Preliminary
chart of
the Atlantic
coast from
Cape
Hatteras
to Cape
Florida.
Autographic
transfer
1861. *Library
of Congress.*

Top: Aerial view of the Cape Florida Lighthouse in Key Biscayne, a barrier island town across the Rickenbacker Causeway from Miami, Florida. *Library of Congress, Carol M. Highsmith.*

Bottom: United States Light-House Establishment outline map showing districts and a few important lights. *Library of Congress.*

BETWEEN 1840 AND 1940, there was a boom in the construction of lighthouses, and in the United States, the number of lighthouses surged from 16 to roughly 1,500 during this time. Though other countries went into a golden age of lighthouse construction during this time, their numbers were far from the popularity of lighthouses in America.

Florida experienced the boom like the rest of the country, and according to the Florida Lighthouse Association, thirty lighthouses remain in full operation along Florida's 1,800-mile coastline.[2] These lighthouses once served as beacons of hope for ships sailing across the Atlantic that they had not been lost at sea and warning messages letting sailors know where they were in relation to the land.

Lighthouses would glow along Florida's coastline from sunset to sunrise, and early lighthouses operated using whale oil and kerosene to produce the light. Later, reflectors were added to magnify the beam, followed by electrical lights and a lens to magnify the light beam. Different lights and flashing colors were used to help sailors identify the lighthouse at night.[3]

The soft sand, hurricanes and high temperatures often made it challenging to build lighthouses along the state's coastal regions. Over time, multiple replacement towers were constructed in the same location after previous lighthouses were destroyed. During the Civil War, the lighthouses became targets and lookout posts, many of which were destroyed.

After the Civil War, new technology, including the skeletal steel tower, permitted the construction of more lighthouse-style structures. As a result, many of the remaining lighthouses are open to the public and serve as centerpieces in state and national parks.

Haunted Florida Lighthouses takes you on a journey into the universe of lighthouses and what life was like as a keeper, which may offer a better understanding of why these structures are several of the most haunted places in Florida. This book covers the St. Augustine Lighthouse, Jupiter Inlet Lighthouse, Ponce de Leon Inlet Lighthouse and Key West Lighthouse.

1

WHY ARE LIGHTHOUSES HAUNTED?

The meagre lighthouse all in white, haunting the seaboard, as if it were the ghost of an edifice that had once had colour and rotundity, dripped melancholy tears after its late buffeting by the waves.
—*Charles Dickens*

Today, the idea of researching paranormal activity has become a popular one among researchers, investigators, tourists and anyone interested in learning more about this type of unexplainable phenomenon. Though many research and investigate haunted locations to discover more about what happens when we enter the afterlife, some enjoy visiting haunted locations for the thrill. These people we refer to as paranormal tourists are an essential part of the paranormal field.

Spirits and paranormal entities do not act on command, and because of this, you never know when paranormal activity may be captured. Working with and relying on those who visit the haunted location as paranormal tourists may be the key to finding the truth behind the answers we, as paranormal researchers, seek.

Lighthouses are popular locations for paranormal tourists to explore and investigate. But why a lighthouse? Lighthouses, especially those in Florida, have a long history of devastation, destruction, love, compassion and trauma imprinted on these structures and the land they tower over.

Lighthouses serve coastal regions as beacons of light, safety and hope, often meaning the difference between life and death at sea. So many seafarers would have been lost at sea in the dark of night or the chaos of an incoming violent storm. As more ships were lost at sea, Congress approved a commission to erect lighthouses in dangerous coastal regions. When Congress did not approve the construction of a lighthouse, the locals often banded together to raise funds to erect a lighthouse and keep their shores safe against dangerous waters.

Unfortunately, lighthouses did not always succeed in the job they were meant to do. Several captains, sailors and passengers died from coastal accidents, pirate attacks and other incidents resulting from the lack of light from the coastal beacons they relied on.

The many deaths and traumatic events on the shores where lighthouses stood watch are believed to be the number one reason lighthouses are haunted. Still, the truth behind the paranormal activity at these lighthouses of hope goes far beyond the deaths that may have and do occur in these areas of Florida.

Additionally, lighthouse keepers lived a life of isolation, fear and uncertainty while being relied on to handle the massive responsibility of maintaining and operating the lighthouse tower and surrounding grounds. As a result, many keepers became attached to their duties and are believed to continue their work in the afterlife. In contrast, other paranormal activity is believed to be tied to other traumatic events the lighthouse keepers and their families experienced while living a life of isolation and separation from society.

It is not uncommon to visit a lighthouse and experience one form of paranormal experience or another. Because of this, paranormal tourists flock to lighthouses in the hopes of having a personal experience or capturing the next critical piece of evidence to share with the community. Paranormal researchers are also interested in learning why lighthouses are so haunted and conduct various experiments to determine if the lighthouse tower, nearby waterways or other factors influence the paranormal activity in lighthouse towers, nearby keepers' dwellings or the surrounding land areas.

Common paranormal experiences in and around lighthouses include rapping, knocking, cold spots, creaking sounds and odd noises. Though several natural elements, including wildlife trapped in the lighthouse tower, structural deterioration and outside influences, can lead many to believe a lighthouse is haunted, there are other cases where the lighthouses are plagued with spirits from the other side.

The spirits encountered at lighthouses throughout Florida have included those of pirates, lighthouse keepers, families, children, boaters, fishermen and others who have visited and died in the area near the lighthouses. However, death near a lighthouse is not the sole reason lighthouses are haunted.

Lighthouses were often visited by those seeking a quiet place to enjoy while on vacation, and many loved being near the beauty of the lighthouse and the waters they stand guard over. Because their visit to a lighthouse was a good time, it is possible that many of those who visited Florida lighthouses returned in the afterlife to enjoy one of the favorite times of their lives.

Even skeptical paranormal researchers experience strange activity when visiting and researching lighthouses. Everything from seeing apparitions to having vivid dreams about a lighthouse they have never visited, unexplainable phenomena and disembodied voices have turned even the most skeptical researcher into a believer after visiting a lighthouse.

Many places believed to be haunted worldwide have been left in disrepair. Still, luckily, a majority of Florida lighthouses have been restored and adequately taken care of, offering a safe place for researchers to investigate and capture paranormal evidence.

One theory, which is possible in some older locations, is that paranormal experiences are related to hallucinations. For example, hallucinations are possible in connection with gas lamps, which are common in older lighthouses. Experiencing hallucinations in older structures where gas lamps are used is also referred to as "Haunted House Syndrome," which occurs when exposed to carbon monoxide poisoning, common in structures dating back to the 1920s.

Though there are several natural occurrences and explanations for experiencing paranormal encounters, some incidents cannot be explained by natural circumstances or other items related to the location's environment.

Some unexplainable incidents where paranormal activity cannot be explained may include death at a location, traumatic events imprinting on the environment or other events with a strong psychic connection to the lighthouse environment.

Additionally, an activity repeated at the same time every day, month or year can create a psychic imprint on the environment that will last for many generations after. For example, the lighthouse keeper ascends the spiral staircase to the top of the lighthouse to light the beacon used to warn ships approaching the dangerous shores. This daily routine could eventually imprint on the environment. Long after the keeper has left his station or died, others in the lighthouse tower can hear his footsteps ascending up the tower as if he were performing his daily routine.

In this example, the sounds of the lighthouse keeper's footsteps could be considered a residual haunting, which is the paranormal activity that occurs at the same time and place (daily, monthly or yearly) and, when approached by the living, does not intelligently interact with those observing the paranormal event.

There is another theory about why paranormal activity can occur in a location, especially in older lighthouses. Many paranormal researchers believe that a site undergoing renovations or repairs can release paranormal activity into the environment. Others believe that the spirits behind protecting the lighthouses get upset when renovations begin and make their presence known by upsetting and scaring those working on the upgrades. Most researchers believe that spirits get upset when the home or structure they love so much is being changed during renovations. They will do everything possible to show their disapproval or stop the upgrades altogether.

Another theory is that the old designs, structures and history contribute to paranormal investigators' eerie feelings when visiting a lighthouse and can eventually make the investigator uneasy. These feelings of unrest when investigating dilapidated and abandoned lighthouses could make a paranormal researcher start to experience strange occurrences, including supernatural entities with sinister and evil motives, which are self-manifested by the investigator's fears.

Ultimately, the paranormal activity tied to the traumatic events at these lighthouses can lead a person to realize that the Sunshine State was not always sunny.

Only one question remains: "Are all lighthouses haunted?"

The answer for this would be no, but that does not mean they are not haunted. There are several reasons why there may not be reports of paranormal activity at several lighthouses in the world. First, no one may have had an experience because the spirits remain hidden. Second, the lighthouse may not be visited enough to discover spirits lurking in the shadows. Third, some people who have experienced paranormal activity at a location may not share their stories for fear of being thought crazy. Fourth, some locations require paranormal investigators to sign a nondisclosure agreement, restricting them from sharing any experiences, stories or evidence related to their paranormal investigation at the lighthouse.

However, it is believed that a majority of the lighthouses in Florida have reports of paranormal activity.

2
FLORIDA LIGHTHOUSES

Love is a lighthouse: it shines through darkest fears
and helps you get where you want to be.
—Janet Todd

L ighthouses in Florida have come and gone throughout history. Everything from hurricanes to beach erosion and lack of care to lack of funds has led to the destruction and extinguishing of lighthouses along the coast of the Sunshine State. Today, there are thirty lighthouses still standing and performing their intended duties in Florida. Several other lighthouses still stand but are no longer used to illuminate Florida's coastline. Many lighthouses along the more than 1,800 miles of Florida coastline are still operating, and others have been named historical landmarks or part of a state or national park.

Florida has the longest stretch of land protected by lighthouses than any other state and is home to some of the nation's tallest and oldest lighthouse structures. Many lighthouses in Florida have been beautifully maintained, and others have undergone significant renovations and restorations, bringing their former glory back to light. Many lighthouses are open to the public, some are available to see at a state park and others are only accessible to view or visit by boat.

Lighthouse enthusiasts enjoy exploring and visiting the many towers in Florida, and several enjoy what many refer to as the "Florida Lighthouse Trail." This trail includes visiting lighthouses starting on the northeast coast of Florida, following down the Atlantic Ocean to the Florida Keys and then back up the West Coast following the Gulf of Mexico through the Panhandle.

Many of these lighthouses are covered in detail throughout this book, including those where paranormal activity has been reported and has become a way of life for those who work at and visit the lighthouse tower and surrounding property.

Famous lighthouses throughout the state of Florida, including some that have been destroyed, replaced or extinguished, include:

St. Augustine Lighthouse and Maritime Museum
Ponce de Leon Inlet Lighthouse and Museum
Jupiter Inlet Lighthouse and Museum
Cape Florida Lighthouse
Key West Lighthouse and Museum
Port Boca Grande Lighthouse
Gasparilla Island Lighthouse
Egmont Key Lighthouse
St. Marks Lighthouse
Pensacola Lighthouse and Maritime Museum
Amelia Island Lighthouse
Cape Canaveral Lighthouse
Hillsboro Inlet Lighthouse
Cape San Blas Lighthouse
Tortugas Harbor Lighthouse
Garden Key Lighthouse
Crooked River Lighthouse
Cape St. George Lighthouse
Cedar Zola's Lighthouse
Alligator Reef Lighthouse
Sanibel Lighthouse
Carysfort Lighthouse
Key Largo Lighthouse

More about many of these lighthouses is included in this book, along with information about their unique history, legends and the paranormal activity within the walls of the lighthouse towers.

3

St. Augustine Lighthouse

St. Augustine, Florida

In the realm of flower a perfumed land, Girt by the sea,
by soft winds fanned; Stands the quaint old Spanish city…
—*Henry Wadsworth Longfellow*

St. Augustine Lighthouse is the oldest lighthouse in the country and has become an icon in Florida's culture and history.[4] This lighthouse was the first to be built in Florida under the new American government when John Adams bought almost the entire state of Florida from the Spanish government. Adams had plans to remodel and renovate the state to make it available for tourists, bringing in money to the local economy.

Initially, the site was the location of a watchtower built by the Spaniards to help prevent pirate attacks. From 1822 to 1867, the watchtower slowly evolved into the lighthouse it is today. At first, this lighthouse used a system of lamps and reflector panels, but the light was still challenging to see from the sea.

It was not until 1822 when French engineer Augustin-Jean Fresnel perfected the Fresnel lens, which changed the production of modern optics forever. However, due to the expense of changing lenses in lighthouses, St. Augustine's light tower was raised ten feet in 1852 to improve visibility instead of changing the lenses for a new Fresnel lens.

In 1853, the lighthouse was finally updated with a new Fresnel lens, which used a single lard oil lamp with whale oil for fuel.

Left: The St. Augustine Lighthouse stands tall, overlooking the many ghosts who call this impressive structure home. *Philip R. Wyatt.*

Right: The St. Augustine Lighthouse, officially Light Station, completed in 1874 in St. Augustine, Florida. *Library of Congress, Carol M. Highsmith.*

The lighthouse stands 164 feet tall where the Matanzas and Tolomato Rivers spill into the Atlantic Ocean on Anastasia Island.

During the American Civil War, Confederate sympathizers in St. Augustine eliminated the illuminating glow on the coast by removing the lens and clockwork. They hid these items to block Union shipping efforts in the area.

The lighthouse keeper's house was added in 1876 and is one of the most paranormal active locations on the property. Several visitors have reported feeling unexplained cold spots and seeing the apparition of a tall, slender man staring at them from the corner of the room.

A suspicious fire ravaged the lighthouse keeper's home, which was vacant at the time because it was declared unnecessary by the government. The Junior Service League stepped in to save the landmark from being demolished, and it is now listed on the National Register of Historic Places and home to a maritime museum.

Unfortunately, an angry spirit caused chaos during the restoration of the lighthouse keeper's home. This evil spirit attempted to get the workers to

Top: Small entrance building beneath the St. Augustine Lighthouse, officially Light Station, completed in 1874 in St. Augustine, Florida. *Library of Congress, Carol M. Highsmith.*

Bottom: The keeper's house at the St. Augustine Lighthouse, officially Light Station, completed in 1874 in St. Augustine, Florida. *Library of Congress, Carol M. Highsmith.*

leave by causing all sorts of poltergeist-type activity. Some were scared, and others ignored it and continued working.

As one of the oldest remaining structures in the country, it is no wonder why the St. Augustine Lighthouse is one of the most haunted lighthouses in America.[5] The St. Augustine Lighthouse has witnessed many disasters, including devastating hurricanes and endless shipwrecks, such as the sixteen British ships in St. Augustine evacuating troops from the battles of the American Revolution wrecked just off the coast in 1782.

The St. Augustine Lighthouse holds memories of the past, and spirits are attracted to this light beacon. But unfortunately, paranormal activity did not wait to start revealing its presence—strange occurrences date to the new lighthouse's construction in 1871.

View from the St. Augustine Lighthouse, officially Light Station, completed in 1874 in St. Augustine, Florida. *Library of Congress, Carol M. Highsmith.*

Hezekiah H. Pittee, the overseer of the new construction project, often brought his children to the job site with him. Sadly, on July 10, 1873, the kids were playing in a work car that toppled over, crashing into the coast with them inside. Eliza (thirteen) and Mary (fifteen), the oldest Pittee children, drowned in the accident.

Staff and visitors claim to see the playful spirits of the children still having fun inhabiting the lighthouse. Strange occurrences believed to be caused by these spirits include unexplainably locked doors, disembodied laughs and music boxes in the lighthouse that will turn on and pop open when no one is around.

Several people have reported seeing the faces of young girls peeking out of the windows when no one is in the building. Others have heard girlish laughter near the swings, and one person claimed to have seen the apparition of a small girl playing on the swings.

Activity picks up when guests are touring the lighthouse; many guides claim they have more experiences, especially of being touched, when giving a tour. Employees also remember locking the door at the top of the lighthouse tower, but the door is wide open when they come to work the following day.

The spirits at St. Augustine Lighthouse are not shy. Several visitors have shared ghostly reports of seeing the apparition of a young woman dressed in period clothing looking out of the lighthouse windows. Visitors who have encountered this spirit claim she is friendly, and it was an enjoyable experience.

One unique spirit that roams the grounds of the St. Augustine Lighthouse is what people refer to as "The Man in Blue." This apparition appears to

Left: Image from a display at the St. Augustine Lighthouse of three girls, two of whom died while playing at the St. Augustine Lighthouse. *Philip R. Wyatt.*

Right: Image of a window at the St. Augustine Lighthouse where there are reports of apparitions looking out. *Philip R. Wyatt.*

workers, wreaking havoc and making their workday a living hell. One worker walked off the job and refused to return after he was reportedly harassed all night by this malevolent spirit.

Some people believe that this spirit is that of Joseph Andreu, the old lighthouse keeper who plummeted to his death while painting the tower in 1859. Others claim this spirit is that of another keeper who was so broken by the consistent solitude of the job that he hanged himself inside the tower.

Visitors and staff claim to smell cigar smoke on the tower's landing, and strange boot steps are heard walking the stairs. The smoke scent is believed to be created by one of the lighthouse's first keepers, Peter Rasmussen, who loved a good cigar.

A woman is also spotted at the top of the lighthouse, often caught from the corner of the eye. She appears to be looking over the railing and then disappears when someone looks straight at her. It is also believed this is the apparition seen looking over the railing at the top of the spiral staircase leading to the top of the lighthouse. In addition, some paranormal researchers have captured video and photo evidence of this apparition looking over the railing when shooting from the lighthouse's base.

This page, top: Image of the stairwell inside the St. Augustine Lighthouse. *Philip R. Wyatt.*

This page, bottom: Spiral staircase inside the St. Augustine Lighthouse, officially Light Station, completed in 1874 in St. Augustine, Florida. *Library of Congress, Carol M. Highsmith.*

Opposite: St. Augustine Lighthouse. *Philip R. Wyatt.*

There are several theories behind the woman who is seen lurking in the lighthouse tower, and many paranormal researchers believe it is the spirit of Maria Mestre de los Dolores. In 1859, she became the first woman to serve in the U.S. Coast Guard and the first Hispanic American woman to command a federal shore installation at the St. Augustine Lighthouse.

The death of her husband, Andreu, left her heartbroken, and she was known for standing at the edge of the catwalk looking down at where her husband's body landed after his horrific accident.

There is no doubt that the St. Augustine Lighthouse holds the memories of the former lighthouse keepers, their families and those who relied on the tower's light. Stories of paranormal activity are everywhere on this property, including where the keepers laid their heads, cigar smoke–filled stairwells and apparitions of former residents living as usual.

St. Augustine Lighthouse. *Philip R. Wyatt.*

The basement is believed to be haunted by a male entity who is believed to have killed himself on the property. This entity may be attached or tied to something on display in the museum's basement.

Another tall male entity has been spotted wearing a gray military uniform standing in the video room's doorway, walking across the lawn and hanging around the cistern. The chairs in the video room seem to be rearranged and often overturned overnight to be discovered the following day.

The second floor of the lightkeepers' home has a lot of activity, including the sound of voices and footsteps when no one is up there. When a guest of the keeper stayed on the second floor, he was suddenly woken up in the early morning hours by a young girl, about thirteen to fifteen, standing at his bedside. The young girl was wearing a long dress and stared at him until she slowly faded away.

There is paranormal activity near the back of the lighthouse, which could be considered residual energy. Residual energy is the paranormal activity that repeats as if a recorded video. This female tends to go about her business, not responding to anyone or anything in the area.

Philip Wyatt, the founder of Georgia Paranormal Investigations, has investigated the St. Augustine Lighthouse several times, and during one visit, it was apparent the spirits wanted to communicate. While visiting the lightkeeper's home, Wyatt captured several EVPs (electronic voice phenomenon) of spirits wishing him to know they were there.

EVPs captured during his investigation included "Hi!" "Mommy here?" and "Hey." When he was leaving and saying his goodbyes, he caught a clear EVP saying "Goodbye" in return.

Two additional notable deaths[6] at the St. Augustine Lighthouse believed to contribute to the paranormal activity are lighthouse keeper William Ham, who died of tuberculosis on April 1, 1889, and Kate Ham, William Ham's wife, who became keeper after his death and died on September 21, 1894.

Today, the St. Augustine Lighthouse & Maritime Museum is open to the public and is part of the National Register of Historic Places. The lighthouse is still active, serving as a beacon for those out at sea off the shores of Florida.

4

JUPITER INLET LIGHTHOUSE
AND MUSEUM

JUPITER, FLORIDA

The light that shines in the darkness, and the darkness can never extinguish it.
—John 1:5 (NLT)

The Jupiter Inlet Lighthouse is the most popular tourist attraction in the area and is known for its many ghostly visitors.

The lighthouse was built in 1860, and this towering landmark is believed to stand on a Native American burial ground. However, there is no significant evidence this is true.

During construction, the lighthouse was built on a natural sand dune, used as a meeting place for ancient Indian tribes for thousands of years. The 105-foot tower is set 145 feet above sea level, and the glow from the light can be seen for 25 nautical miles. The Jupiter Inlet Lighthouse is a significant part of Florida's history and an impressive sight from land and sea.

Paranormal activity experienced at the Jupiter Inlet Lighthouse includes strange noises, disembodied voices and ghostly hands touching a person's shoulders. Some paranormal researchers believe the activity is tied to a former lighthouse keeper. Still, the paranormal activity at this east coast lighthouse could be caused by one of many historical events.

Visitors and employees claim to hear strange noises and feel the sensation of being touched on the shoulder and hand. Others have reported feeling cold spots, but the building is very drafty, so this is not any verifiable form of paranormal evidence.

Left: Jupiter Inlet
Lighthouse. *Library of
Congress, George Baker.*

Below: Jupiter Inlet
as seen from atop of
the lighthouse. *Library
of Congress, William
Henry Jackson.*

There is a heavy presence in the gift shop, and even though there haven't been sightings of apparitions in this area, many feel sadness when walking into the gift shop.

So, who or what is haunting the Jupiter Inlet Lighthouse? One story shares a face-to-face encounter with an apparition near the top of the lighthouse stairs. The guest reported seeing a tall figure appear instantly in front of her with dark eye sockets and a gaping mouth. The upper half of the body was clear, but the lower portion was a fuzzy white mass.

Jupiter Inlet Light, first lit in 1860, was erected on a prehistoric Indian mound, Jupiter, Florida. *Library of Congress, Carol M. Highsmith.*

The guest claims the figure reached out to her with a bony hand, and she lost track of time and did not remember what happened next until her friends woke her up.

This figure could have been that of lighthouse keeper Joseph Wells, buried in the small graveyard adjacent to the keeper's house. Buried with Wells are his wife, Katherine, and their stillborn children.

Additional accounts of unexplained occurrences at the Jupiter Inlet Lighthouse include hearing footsteps, disembodied voices and strange sounds in the lighthouse when no one else is there.

5

PORT BOCA GRANDE LIGHTHOUSE

BOCA GRANDE, FLORIDA

Darkness reigns at the foot of the lighthouse.
—Japanese proverb

Built in 1890, the Port Boca Grande Lighthouse was initially planned as a safe method to guide ships into Charlotte Harbor. This lighthouse is the only one on the west coast of Florida open to the public and one of six in the entire state.

Today, the Port Boca Grande Lighthouse is home to a museum displaying the rich history of the area and the legends and lore of Gasparilla Island. This family-friendly museum offers a look into the lives of the Calusa Native Americans, the prosperous phosphate industry, Boca Grande Pass and its history with tarpon fishing.

According to Elsie Williams, the granddaughter of William Lester, the lighthouse keeper from 1894 to 1923, many famous people visited Gasparilla Island. Her grandfather invited these famous people to see the lighthouse and enjoy some entertainment. Some of his guests included millionaires John Rockefeller and John Jacob Astor.[7] Lester was accommodating to many in the area, and his entertainment imprinted intense energy on the area, which could be part of why the Port Boca Grande Lighthouse is so haunted.

Some paranormal claims include hearing voices, laughter and music. These sounds could be residual energy recorded on the environment, but they could also be the spirits of those who visited because it was such a happy time in their life.

Another contributing factor behind the paranormal activity at this lighthouse could be the suicide of a young assistant keeper, Charles Fine. Fine was supposed to get married and had been approved for leave on May 1, 1931. He was going to visit his parents with his bride, but for an unknown reason, that never happened.

The wife of keeper Charles Williams heard a gunshot from the lighthouse on April 28. She discovered Fine's body, shot by a contraption he created by hanging the shotgun from the ceiling with an electric light cord while holding the muzzle in one hand and pulling the trigger using a stick.

Fine's body was transported to Key West, where his father, Robert J. Fine, a retired lighthouse keeper, lived.

Some believe Fine is the one haunting the Port Boca Grande Lighthouse, but it could also be some of the other lighthouse keepers refusing to leave their duty of keeping the lighthouse lit.

Several paranormal researchers have claimed there is a spirit of a young girl haunting the lighthouse and Gasparilla Island. Could this girl's spirit be that of a lighthouse keeper's daughter who died in their dwelling? It is unknown what she died of, but during that time, she likely died of diphtheria or whooping cough. Several tour guides and park rangers claim the second-floor room is one of the girl's favorite places to play and is often heard during overnight hours, being most active around midnight. Paranormal reports surrounding this spirit include hearing a child's footsteps and playful laughter.

It is also possible the paranormal activity is the spirit of Josefa, a Spanish princess who was decapitated by José Gaspar, the pirate for whom Gasparilla Island is believed to be named. Several people have reported seeing the apparition of a headless spirit roaming the grounds, and several believe this specter is of Josefa.

Gaspar buried his treasure in the sand near the lighthouse more than ninety years before it was built. He had fallen in love with Josefa and kidnapped her, but she continually rejected his love. Finally, feeling rejected, Gaspar pulled his sword and cut off the princess's head in a rage. He buried her body in the sand of the island, and because he loved her so much, he continued to carry her head with him for the rest of his life.

Many feel Josefa's headless body remains on Gasparilla Island, searching for her head.

Another popular spirit at the lighthouse is a little girl known for sounding happy and being playful. The haunting was discovered during a time when renovations were being completed on the Port Boca Grande

Lighthouse—a little girl would make her presence known by laughing. This spirit is believed to be the daughter of one of the lighthouse keepers who died in the keeper's house from diphtheria or whooping cough. Tour guides share stories about the young girl playing in the room upstairs, and she is typically heard around midnight.

It wasn't until 1956 that the U.S. Coast Guard automated the light of the Port Boca Grande Lighthouse; however, ten years later, the Coast Guard had to remove the light from the building because it was deteriorating due to years of neglect and beach erosion. Luckily, in 1972, Lee County took over ownership of the lighthouse and surrounding land and began the long restoration process to save the structure.

The Port Boca Grande Lighthouse was placed on the National Register of Historic Places in 1980 and was relit and returned to service as a fully functioning Coast Guard light in 1988. That same year, the lighthouse and surrounding land were transferred from Lee County to the State of Florida and renamed Gasparilla Island State Park.

6

PENSACOLA LIGHTHOUSE

PENSACOLA, FLORIDA

In order for the light to shine so brightly, the darkness must also be present.
—Francis Bacon

Built in the 1800s, the Pensacola Lighthouse and Museum is a historic and wonderful gem set in Florida. The lighthouse tower has 177 steps, leading to one of the most spectacular views of Florida's Gulf Coast. The lighthouse and property are magnificent; however, when the sun sets, the property turns into an entirely new environment. The Pensacola Lighthouse is called one of the most haunted lighthouses in America, and several paranormal researchers have unexplainable experiences that can put chills down your spine.

The Pensacola Lighthouse has also had its fair share of being subjected to Mother Nature's wrath. In 1874 and 1875, reports claimed the lighthouse tower was struck by lightning. A rare occurrence followed these lightning strikes in Florida: the lighthouse tower was shaken by an earthquake in 1886, which is mysterious because this region is not often subjected to earthquakes.

Though Florida does not experience many earthquakes, the state has experienced plenty of hurricanes, and the Gulf Coast has been subjected to these massive storms throughout history. However, since the lighthouse sits high up on a hill facing the bay, it has been saved many times from being significantly affected by the high winds, heavy rains and massive waves that come to shore with hurricanes.

These acts of nature could fuel the paranormal activity experienced at the lighthouse and the surrounding grounds.

Pensacola Lighthouse. *Library of Congress, Carol M. Highsmith.*

Several paranormal researchers have experienced strange occurrences and interactions with the spirits that call the Pensacola Lighthouse and Museum home. It is believed that at least six spectral residents are still residing at the lighthouse.[8] However, these ghost hunters are not the only ones who have experienced interactions with unseen entities. Several guests who have taken

Left: Pensacola Lighthouse, San Carlos Road, Pensacola, Escambia County, Florida. *Library of Congress.*

Right: Pensacola Lighthouse, San Carlos Road, Pensacola, Escambia County, Florida. *Library of Congress.*

tours of the lighthouse have reported hearing voices, being touched and experiencing a heavy sensation when walking into different structure rooms.

The spirits in the lighthouse, built in 1826 and rebuilt in 1859, are home to souls that have made it a habit of making their presence known.

One spirit that many visitors and employees have encountered at the Pensacola Lighthouse is sinister and believed to have been a murderer when living. This spirit haunts the living quarters and portions of the tower of the old lighthouse and tends to startle locals, creating a sense of fear. As a result, many who have encountered this spirit refuse to return to the room where they were frightened.

One interesting story that could be fueling paranormal activity is that of the original lighthouse keepers: Michaela Penalber and her husband, Jeremiah Ingraham. The couple moved into the lighthouse in 1826. Though they seemed happy living in paradise, maintaining and operating the lighthouse, their love story worsened, resulting in Jeremiah's death in 1840.

Some urban legends claim that Michaela was abused, while others claim she was jealous of her beloved lighthouse and wanted to care for it all alone.

Pensacola Lighthouse, San Carlos Road, Pensacola, Escambia County, Florida. *Library of Congress.*

One foggy night, she took a knife from the kitchen and sliced Jeremiah to death. Unfortunately, there was a lack of evidence, so she was never charged with his death and spent the remainder of her life caring for the lighthouse she loved so much.

Several paranormal investigators believe that Michaela's death in 1855 did not end her living at the lighthouse. Instead, several people believe she remains at the lighthouse, haunting the historic keeper's quarters. Many consider her spirit the same wicked spirit others have reported in these quarters and the tower. Some theories claim Michaela gets agitated and throws objects at visitors because she wants to be left alone.

Additionally, several visitors claim to have heard a woman's voice calling out to them, using their name, followed by a warning—"I'm watching you." Shortly after, several people felt a presence following them up the stairs of the lighthouse tower and could hear breathing behind them when no one was there.

Another story tied to the Pensacola Lighthouse is that of Ellen Mueller and the activity in her bedroom adjacent to the lighthouse's museum. Ellen grew up at the lighthouse and was married there. Unfortunately, in 1911, she died due to complications during childbirth and bled to death in her room.

Another spirit, believed to be the head keeper in 1877, Sam Lawrence, is often seen among the tower's 15 stories, mainly on the 177-step stairwell. Several people who have visited the lighthouse have seen his spirit or felt his presence when walking up or down the staircase. However, several reports of paranormal activity suggest Lawrence is not alone, as he is joined by many other spirits that remained behind in the lighthouse after their deaths.

Two small children have been known to cause fright among visitors and workers at the lighthouse as they run around the lighthouse, often running

Left: Pensacola Lighthouse, San Carlos Road, Pensacola, Escambia County, Florida. *Library of Congress.*

Right: Pensacola Lighthouse, San Carlos Road, Pensacola, Escambia County, Florida. *Library of Congress.*

through a person, object or wall. The spirits of Lizzy and Joey are believed to be children who died in 1922 from yellow fever. Today they are often seen being playful, having fun, laughing and enjoying the afterlife at the Pensacola Lighthouse.

Additional paranormal activity includes K2 meters going off on tours when in the basement directly related to guides asking questions. Interestingly enough, the basement is where the spirits of Thomas and Raymond, runaway slaves hanged and buried on the lighthouse's property, tend to interact with tour guides, guests and paranormal investigators.

Today, the Pensacola Lighthouse and Museum are in the care of the U.S. Coast Guard, and there is no doubt that the Pensacola Lighthouse is haunted by several spirits of the past refusing to leave. Many spirits roam late at the facilities and have been captured on video, in photographs and in personal experiences by guests participating in the late-night ghost tours.

7

CAPE FLORIDA LIGHTHOUSE

KEY BISCAYNE, FLORIDA

The past is a lighthouse, not a port.
—Russian proverb

When exploring the Key Biscayne shoreline, missing the Cape Florida Lighthouse is impossible. This magnificent structure is a staggering sight and holds the key to unlocking the area's great history.

Before LED navigation and other modern lighting fixtures on vessels, the towering structure of the Cape Florida Lighthouse once helped safely guide mariners and fishermen back to the shore.

Looking back on the history of Key Biscayne, the lighthouse, which was built in 1825, is a beautiful piece of history still standing after the horrific history of Indian attacks, Civil War battles, hurricanes and other harrowing events in Florida's history. Though the structure has survived all these historical events, there is much evidence of wear and tear and damage the lighthouse endured.

The Cape Florida Lighthouse is a recognizable landmark in Bill Baggs Cape Florida State Park, and to this day, the lighthouse is the oldest standing structure in the Miami-Dade County area. If this lighthouse could talk, the stories it would share would be unique enough to blow guests away.

When the lighthouse was first built, it was only sixty-five feet high, with wooden stairs, and was essential to keeping sailors and the area safe against pirates and other invaders that posed dangers to Florida in the 1700s and early 1800s. When the first lighthouse keeper and his family moved

Top: The Cape Florida Lighthouse in Key Biscayne, a barrier island town across the Rickenbacker Causeway from Miami, Florida. *Library of Congress, Carol M. Highsmith.*

Bottom: Cape Florida Light, a lighthouse on Cape Florida at the south end of Key Biscayne in Miami-Dade County, Florida. *Library of Congress, Carol M. Highsmith.*

into the property's cottage, they were the first American family to reside in Key Biscayne.

After climbing the 109 stairs, guests visiting the lighthouse will have a stunning, romantic view of the area. However, those who know the history of the lighthouse and the spirits who reside within often feel like they are not alone at the top of the lighthouse.

One day, eleven years after the lighthouse began operating, the keeper and his family were away on a trip. During their absence, a band of Seminole Indians attacked the lighthouse tower, burning the inside wooden structure and pillaging the cottage. Because there was a continuing threat of Indians attacking, it took many years before the lighthouse was rebuilt and started operating again.

Photograph showing Old Cape Florida Lighthouse, Key Biscayne, Florida, with palm trees, at end of dirt path, in a state of disrepair. *Library of Congress.*

The tragic history involving ongoing damage to the lighthouse and dramatic events occurring on the surrounding land is what has fueled paranormal activity. It could be the source of psychic energy getting imprinted on the environment. Even after Florida seceded from the Union in the 1860s, the lighthouse was in and out of service for more than one hundred years, despite tropical storm damage and damage caused by Confederate sympathizers. The tower was restored and reopened in 1996 during Miami's Centennial Celebration, and it is now listed on the U.S. National Register of Historic Places.

Today, visitors can get more detail about the horrific attacked when they tour the lighthouse, including the replicated keeper's cottage. Though it is not the original cottage, the building is filled with antiques and artifacts, providing a glimpse into the secluded life of the keeper's family before being chased away. Some people have claimed to see shadow figures and apparitions and hear strange sounds while in this space.

Could the energy of the keeper's family be imprinted on the antiques and artifacts? Or could it be something associated with the history of the land? As you all know, in the paranormal world, anything is possible.

8

PONCE DE LEON INLET LIGHTHOUSE

PONCE INLET, FLORIDA

Lighthouses are not just stone, brick, glass and metal. There's a human story at every lighthouse; that's the story I wish to inform you.
—*Elinor DeWire*

After climbing the stairs to Florida's tallest lighthouse, you are treated to magnificent views of the inlet. Though it may seem challenging, climbing the 175-foot tower at Ponce Inlet Light Station and Museum is well worth the effort. Since 1887, this lighthouse has guided mariners along Florida's coast, and the lighthouse named after Spanish explorer Juan Ponce de León was declared a National Historic Landmark in 1998.[9]

Nestled ten miles south of Daytona, this world-famous lighthouse museum offers a treasure trove of experiences for everyone who visits. Plus, some hidden treasures prove to visitors that the paranormal world exists within our world, as many have encountered the spirits of past keepers and their families when exploring the Ponce de Leon Inlet Lighthouse.

The Ponce de Leon Inlet is no stranger to tragic events and has been tied to wars, natural disasters and more. In the area originally known as the Mosquito Inlet, local plantation owners petitioned the territorial government to build a lighthouse in 1830. Unfortunately, the petition by local plantation owners was the beginning of the end of the ebb and flow of the lighthouse's past.

The first lighthouse in the area was constructed on the south side of the Inlet in 1835–36 and included a forty-five-foot tower, which was never

Ponce de Leon Inlet Lighthouse, Ponce Inlet, Florida. *Library of Congress, Carol M. Highsmith.*

illuminated because the oil to light the Winslow Lewis chandelier was never delivered. Then a violent storm undermined the structural integrity of the lighthouse tower, nearly killing keeper William H. Williams and his family.

A few months later, when the family was away, the lighthouse was ransacked by Seminole Indians. However, this was not the end of the tragic circumstances the lighthouse and other structures along the Mosquito Inlet would face.

In April 1836, a strong storm and continued ground erosion around the Mosquito Inlet lighthouse forced it to collapse into the sea. After the collapse, things remained quiet in the area for several years until 1887, when one of the last brick lighthouses in America was constructed on the inlet. The masonry giant was lit using Fresnel lenses and was part of a movement when they started building lighthouses out of brick along the U.S. coastline and the Great Lakes.

During the American Civil War from 1861 to 1865, Mosquito Inlet became a refuge and hiding place for Confederate boats looking for a way to circumvent the Union shipping blockades. On April 12, 1862, Harper's Weekly reported a "Fatal Affair at Mosquito Inlet, Florida," when the Navy Department sent an expedition fleet, including the *Penguin*, commanded by Lieutenant F.A. Budd, and *Henry Andrew*, commanded by W. Mather, into the Mosquito Inlet. Both commanding officers and six other seamen were killed during the conflict with Confederates. Seven other men were wounded in the confrontation.

Another tragic event near the inlet was when a gun-running expedition to Cuba on the steam tug *Commodore* sank about twelve miles off the shores of Daytona in 1897. American author Stephen Crane worked on the *Commodore* as an undercover correspondent for the *New York Post* to bring supplies to Cuba to aid in their rebellion against Spanish rule of the island.

The ship departed in the early morning from Jacksonville, and as it sank, the survivors credited the beacon from the Mosquito Inlet lighthouse guiding them in their rowboats back to shore. Eight men died in the sinking; however, Crane survived and wrote the short story "The Open Boat."

When war broke out again in 1898 during the Spanish American War, the lighthouse was used to hang a halyard on the main balcony to communicate by signal flags with passing American warships as they traveled toward Cuba. Additionally, in 1898, the owner of the land purchased for the Mosquito Inlet Light Station, Bartola Pacetti, died and is buried in the nearby Pacetti Cemetery.

One interesting and unsolved incident that occurred near the Mosquito Inlet lighthouse was when a number of whales were driven ashore near the Mosquito Inlet lighthouse. This was another tragic event that occurred in 1908, for unknown reasons, with the most significant whale measuring forty feet long.

The first assistant lighthouse keeper, Joseph Davis, who died of a heart attack while working the lighthouse in 1919, is believed to be one of the spirits haunting the Ponce de Leon Inlet Lighthouse. Davis died while climbing the lighthouse tower, and several people attribute the scent of kerosene to his spirit—the fuel has not been used in the lighthouse since 1933. However, some believe that the source of the kerosene smell is the old tanks being stored on the property, so this may not be paranormal.

It is also believed that the spirit of a former lightkeeper's son, William Linquist, likes to play pranks at the lighthouse and is known for opening and closing doors. William was the son of an assistant to lighthouse keeper John Linquist.

William died in 1922 from severe injuries he suffered after being kicked by a horse. Light anomalies have been reported around the grounds and are thought to be connected to this boy's spirit.

It was not until 1927 when the Mosquito Inlet was renamed the Ponce de Leon Inlet, and the light station was also renamed to match the name of the inlet it sits on. In April of the same year, the property suffered a major scrub fire and had many renovations completed on the lighthouse tower.

As one can imagine, maintaining and operating a lighthouse can be a lonely job for the keepers and their families. Though the Ponce de Leon Inlet Lighthouse is near Daytona, those who lived and worked there suffered from painful feelings of isolation and depression. The sense of isolation contributed to several suicides and infirmities among those who lived there.

Two of the homes on the property are active and full of spirits, including the presence of a woman who is believed to be one of the female lighthouse keepers or a keeper's wife. In the third house on the property, which is glassed off, a small china doll is believed to be haunted. Many people feel the sensation of being watched, creepy feelings and strange light anomalies in the room with the doll.

Though there are not a significant number of paranormal reports about the Ponce de Leon Inlet Lighthouse and Museum, with its tragic past, there is no doubt something has attached itself to the land, and many of the former lighthouse keepers remain behind continuing with their duties.

9

ST. GEORGE ISLAND LIGHTHOUSE

EASTPOINT, FLORIDA

The sea is as close as we come to another world.
—Anne Stevenson

The St. George Island Lighthouse was a historical treasure on Florida's forgotten coast and tragically collapsed into the Gulf of Mexico on October 21, 2005.[10] Finally, near the end of 2008, the newly reconstructed lighthouse was opened to the public.

So, what was the original lighthouse like, and was it haunted? Is the reconstructed lighthouse also haunted? Continue reading for the answers you seek.

The original St. George Island Lighthouse was built in 1833, rebuilt in 1848 and again in 1852 after the second lighthouse tower collapsed during a hurricane in 1851. The lighthouses were constructed on what is now known as Little St. George Island. After years of beach erosion caused by the pounding waves, the lighthouse finally succumbed and collapsed into the Gulf. State and federal agencies worked to help the St. George Lighthouse Association spearhead an effort to salvage pieces of the light and thousands of old bricks. Then, the original plans were obtained from the National Archives in Washington, D.C., to aid in the reconstruction of the lighthouse with as much of the original materials as possible.

Additionally, the construction of a replica of the original keeper's house started next to the lighthouse in the fall of 2009, and the two-story brick structure opened to the general public in the summer of 2011. The keeper's house held a museum, sharing the story of the lighthouse and its keepers.

Left: Cape Saint George Lighthouse, Cape St. George, Apalachicola, Franklin County, Florida. *Library of Congress*.

Right: Cape Saint George Lighthouse, Cape St. George, Apalachicola, Franklin County, Florida. *Library of Congress*.

During the reconstruction of the lighthouse and the keeper's home, the original granite door jambs and window lintels were reinstalled, and the iron lantern room was reforged using original pieces as patterns.

With such an exciting history involving several lighthouse structures falling to their demise, there is no wonder the St. George Island Lighthouse is haunted. Unfortunately, many lighthouse visitors and Florida residents do not realize that the St. George Island Lighthouse is shrouded by a mysterious, dark history and is home to many paranormal and supernatural entities.

Paranormal investigators who have had the opportunity to investigate the St. George Island Lighthouse and the keeper's home have reported many ghostly encounters. Everyday paranormal activity includes the sensation of being watched, getting touched and hearing strange noises throughout both structures on the island.

During EVP sessions, paranormal researchers captured male and female voices, strange noises and crying. Many of the EVP captures were intelligent answers to direct questions during a paranormal investigation.

One interesting story about St. George Island might not have to deal directly with the lighthouse. Still, it could have a significant impact on

Cape Saint George Lighthouse, Cape St. George, Apalachicola, Franklin County, Florida. *Library of Congress.*

the paranormal activity experienced on the island and in and around the lighthouse.

Florida natives share stories associated with a local legend about a coven of witches called St. George Island home a long time ago. The island was where these witches performed seances and rituals in peace, away from others who were believed to persecute them. However, residents in the area were less pleased to know a coven was actively practicing close to their homes and families.

While strolling through the woods searching for herbs, a fourteen-year-old girl close to being initiated into the coven was attacked by a group of young men. The young men threw rocks at her until she fell, leaving her bruised and mentally broken on the cold hard ground. When questioned, the men claim they only tried to protect the island.

Shaken, the girl stumbled home, telling her mother, a witch, about the incident, which filled the mom with blind rage. She managed to find the location where her daughter was attacked in the woods and tracked the boys by their footprints back to the tavern, where she found them drinking. The witch stormed into the tavern and openly placed a curse on the young men, casting an evil spell on them.

Fear filled the hearts of the locals, who rallied together and arrested every member of the coven. Since she was not yet a member of the coven, the teenage girl vowed to protect forever the young women living on the island moments before she killed herself. Watching and protecting the women who visit and explore the island was a vow the budding witch is believed to have honored.

One story shared online is of a young girl exploring the island and being approached by two guys who appeared out of the darkness and laughing.[11] The guys stopped in her way, grinning at her in a way that she claims made her feel uncomfortable, and her skin crawled. She tried to run away but was grabbed and tossed to the ground while one of the guys pinned her arms down.

Thinking the men would rape her, she looked off into the distance and saw a black-cloaked figure appear. The moment the figure appeared, the men started crying in pain and suddenly fled into the night.

This girl did not know about the witches of St. George Island but believed it was the young girl's spirit holding up her promise to protect females in danger while on the island.

Though there is not much information about the witches on the island or recent occurrences with the cloaked figure, it is possible that paranormal activity related to these events can occur anywhere on the island, including at the lighthouse.

10

HILLSBORO INLET LIGHTHOUSE

HILLSBORO BEACH, FLORIDA

No lighthouse can assist you if you close your eyes!
—Mehmet Murat Ildan

The Hillsboro Inlet Lighthouse is set on the site as part of a large land grant issued by the English Crown to Wills Hill, the Earl of Hillsborough. Hills was Britain's secretary of state for the colonies from 1766 until 1772, and the beach, inlet and lighthouse still carry the earl's name (though a shortened version) to this day. Though the lighthouse has an aristocratic heritage and today is part of the Millionaire's Mile, it is still possible to get a decent view of the lighthouse without showing proof of your multimillions of dollars.

The dangerous waters surrounding the reef in the Hillsboro Inlet forced ships to take a wide berth, often going out into the Gulf Stream. Therefore, it was requested a light be put in place to help vessels from the Bahama Banks to verify their position in the event they failed to make the Jupiter Inlet. The Hillsboro Inlet Lighthouse was the light that would complete the system of lights on the Florida Reefs.

The original site selected south of the current inlet was found unsuitable for supporting the foundation of a lighthouse. But they still wanted to build a lighthouse, and with the money provided by the government, three acres of swampland north of the inlet was purchased, and the 137-foot-tall octagonal tower was ordered to be built. The lighthouse tower was officially lit on March 7, 1907, by Alfred Alexander Berghell, the first head keeper at the Hillsboro Inlet Lighthouse.

Hillsboro Inlet Light is located on the north side of Hillsboro Inlet, midway between Fort Lauderdale and Boca Raton, in Hillsboro Beach, Florida. *Library of Congress, Carol M. Highsmith.*

In September 1926, a hurricane struck the lighthouse station, causing the tower to vibrate and forcing the mercury used to float the lens to slosh around and out of its troughs. The incandescent oil vapor lamp was broken from this incident, and the lighthouse structure's foundation was exposed to a depth of eight feet. Homes in the area were destroyed, and fifteen people were given refuge at the station during the remainder of the storm. Ten years later, in 1936, another hurricane swept through the region, destroying the head lighthouse keeper's dwelling.

The Barefoot Mailman was a term used for letter carriers between 1885 and 1892. These letter carriers would travel the sixty-eight-mile-long coastline from Miami to Palm Beach primarily by foot along the hard sand near the water's edge. When the mail carrier approached the Hillsboro Inlet, he would use a small rowboat to cross the inlet waters. James E. "Ed" Hamilton was the most remembered Barefoot Mailman.

One Hillsboro Inlet Lighthouse urban legend involves the Barefoot Mailman, and it is believed that Hamilton died in an attempt to reach the lighthouse for a routine mail delivery. In October 1887, he was not feeling well but still insisted on completing his duties of delivering the mail to the lighthouse. So he traveled south along his route to the lighthouse but failed to return as expected.

Worried, two of Hamilton's friends headed out to look for him, and upon their arrival at the Hillsboro Inlet, they discovered the mailman's mail pouch, shirt and trousers hanging on a tree limb, but Hamilton was nowhere in sight.

It is believed that a stranger stumbled upon the rowboat and used it to leave the area, forcing the Barefoot Mailman to swim across the inlet. Though Hamilton was an excellent swimmer, his friends believed he fell victim to alligators or sharks. His friends spotted tracks of alligators in the area and think they were responsible for their beloved friend's disappearance.[12]

Today, there is a Barefoot Mailman statue overlooking the inlet along with several other monuments and museum-like structures, such as the flagpole, fog bell and plaque, honoring those who served at the Hillsboro Lighthouse.

Though the story of the Barefoot Mailman predates the construction of the lighthouse, it is a vital part of the inlet's history, and it would be interesting to see if he walks the shores trying to continue his mail route. There were no reports of paranormal activity at the lighthouse and surrounding areas, but this could be in part because visitors are allowed to access the Hillsboro Inlet Lighthouse only once a month. With such limited access, paranormal activity may occur, but no one is around to see it.

The Hillsboro Inlet Lighthouse may not have stories recalling paranormal encounters; this lighthouse belongs in this book because the history associated with the lighthouse and the surrounding land makes it a prime candidate to be a haunted location.

So, is the Hillsboro Inlet Lighthouse haunted? Anything is possible!

11

KEY WEST LIGHTHOUSE

KEY WEST, FLORIDA

Metaphysics is a dark ocean without coasts or lighthouses, scattered with numerous philosophic wrecks.
—Immanuel Kant

K ey West, Florida, has been a victim of many hurricanes, some mild and others more severe; however, the worst hurricane on record that struck the Keys was the Havana Hurricane of 1846. Though there is no consensus on the number of deaths caused by the hurricane that year, it is believed about 1,500 people settled in Key West at the time. At least 60 people were known to have perished in the storm, and some of their spirits have been spotted wandering and haunting Key West.

After the Havana Hurricane rampaged through the Keys, only eight buildings remained standing after it returned to the sea. One witness of the aftermath of the Hurricane of 1846 described the scene of Key West as grotesque. When the waters receded, bodies littered the land from the victims who drowned or were hit by debris.

Additionally, among the victims of the hurricane, several coffins and corpses were discovered that had been unearthed from the Whitehead Point Cemetery. The storm moved bones and bodies, distributing them into unexpected sites throughout the island. The exact number of deaths and disturbed graves is still unknown, but the trauma from this single natural disaster is enough to fuel the many phantom mysteries and paranormal events of Key West.

Two Key West lighthouses fell and crumbled into the sea during the hurricane of 1846, killing the people who fled to the towers seeking refuge. As a result, both of these locations are haunted today by paranormal activity, disembodied voices and apparitions.

The Key West Lighthouse keeper, Barbara Mabrity, was an unconventional choice for the job. Still, she spent over thirty-eight years keeping the light on and maintaining the property after her husband died of yellow fever. Though her husband was initially hired for the job, she worked hard to prove she could be the keeper of the lighthouse and started her career as a lighthouse keeper upon his death a few years after he took on the role.

In 1846, when the hurricane hit the Florida Keys, Mabrity and her six children took refuge in the Key West Lighthouse tower. They took shelter from the unforgiving winds and heavy rain along with a few other panicked residents. Unfortunately, the tower did not hold up well against the storm, and the entire structure collapsed.

When the storm passed, bodies were found littered throughout the area where the lighthouse tower once stood. Somehow, Mabrity survived the storm, but her six children did not.

When Florida seceded from the Union in early 1861, Key West was isolated from the happenings of the mainland and its affairs. Key West residents often relied on various federal institutions, such as the Army, Navy, Customs Service, Revenue Cutter Service and Lighthouse Service. Mabrity faithfully maintained lighthouse operations even though the Confederates extinguished all other Florida lighthouses to prevent the Union from safely making it to the state's coastline.

During the Civil War, Mabrity was nearly eighty years old, and the requirements to keep the lighthouse operational were daunting, especially when she had to oversee the new keeper's quarters, a much larger lighthouse and all associated outbuildings on the property. She was also in charge of offering certain aids to navigation for vessels in Key West waters.

In 1862, Mabrity was accused of harboring Southern sympathies, and though she denied these allegations, she was encouraged to retire by the service. She refused to quit, and two years later, she decided it was time to retire at the age of eighty-two and agreed to give up her post as lighthouse keeper of the Key West Lighthouse. Three years later, Mabrity was physically exhausted after close to forty years of service, and she died.

After losing her entire family during a storm, she was forever tied to the land by her grief. Then, shortly after her death, she was believed to appear on the property of the lighthouse, along with other spirits of the hurricane victims.

Today, the Key West Lighthouse is a museum with outstanding views of the Key West area. The museum is filled with various items and allows visitors to see the keeper's quarters, historical memorabilia and a few ghosts who still reside at the lighthouse. Thousands of visitors visit the Key West Lighthouse annually for the history and stunning views of the area. Some of these visitors have shared encounters with ghosts who remain behind in the lighthouse.

One visitor was climbing the eighty-eight steps to the top of the lighthouse tower when she suddenly felt someone behind her. She knew others were touring the lighthouse simultaneously and thought it was one of them, but when she turned around, no one was there. So she kept climbing the staircase, and when she reached the top, she felt the cold wind, which was odd because it was eighty-five degrees that day.

Unsure where the cold air came from, she stood at the window enjoying the view and returned down the stairs. Before leaving the top of the stairs, she felt like an unseen person had hugged her. She saw she was still alone and did not feel threatened because the hug felt like someone wanted to comfort her.

Another visitor shared a similar story but saw something during her lighthouse tour. Before heading up the staircase, the tour guide showed the group around the lower level of the lighthouse tower. During this part of the tour, the woman felt a hand playfully brush her hair, and when she looked at the couple next to her, she knew it was not them.

As the tour continued, her hair was touched again, and she heard a playful laugh. She asked the couple beside her if they felt a breeze, and they said they had not. She did not want others to think she was crazy and opted to keep her experiences to herself. As the tour climbed the stairs, the guest looked to her left and saw what she believed was the ghost of lighthouse keeper Barbara Mabrity.

Several visitors have also seen the spirit of what is believed to be Mabrity walking up the stairs of the lighthouse and then fading away as she ascends to the top. Based on the stairwell spirit's actions, paranormal researchers believe this is a residual haunting, replaying the events Mabrity did day after day as keeper of the lighthouse. She is also thought to be roaming the grounds of the lighthouse property searching for her family.

Mabrity's ghost is only one of many visitors have claimed to see when visiting and touring the Key West Lighthouse. Some people have claimed to see an apparition called Mary and her husband within the keeper's quarters. It is believed these two have come down with typhoid fever while working at the lighthouse and died in the room they are seen in.

Mabrity's granddaughter Mary Armanda Fletcher followed in her grandmother's footsteps and served as assistant keeper of the lighthouse from 1866 until 1889 when she took over the duties as head lighthouse keeper upon the death of her husband, John Carroll. Carroll had died a few days after contracting typhoid fever, and though Mary took over his primary duties, she died three months later from the same ailment.

When they passed, the couple was in the keeper's quarters, and many believe they are two of the many apparitions spotted at the Key West Lighthouse.

Additionally, several other lighthouse staff members have died from typhoid fever. Some believe the lighthouse had its own "Typhoid Mary" who cooked for staff members, spreading the disease to others.

The spirits of two young girls are spotted holding hands and walking or skipping through the grass of the lighthouse grounds. The girls are believed to be two of lighthouse keeper Mabrity's children who died during the hurricane of 1846. These spirits are friendly but never engage or interact with the living, which is why some believe these apparitions are residual energy imprinted from when the girls lived and played on the island.

Another spooky encounter visitors to the Key West Lighthouse have had include a spirit dressed as a soldier guarding the front door. Visitors claim this spirit looks very angry as people pass him and enter through the front door of the lighthouse.

No one knows who this soldier could be, and there are no official records of who he could be. Some believe this spirit is one of the locals who sought shelter during the hurricane, and his uniform appears to be from around the Civil War, which means this entity could be anyone from this time in history. Though this spirit seems angry, those encountering him do not feel threatened. Instead, they feel as if he is watching over things and making sure no one causes harm to the lighthouse.

Other paranormal encounters at the Key West Lighthouse include sightings of a woman believed to be Mabrity standing on the edge of the water as if she is waiting or looking out for the next storm, reports of a phantom couple that, when noticed, fade away and a disoriented male spirit who staggers away and vanishes when approached.

Who is the mysterious phantom couple? Could it be the Mabritys? And could the children's spirits be the Mabrity children who died during the Havana Hurricane?

Another theory about the child spirits is that they are the children from the Native American communities in southern Florida the Spanish disrupted.

Anything is possible.

Sand Key Lighthouse, Sand Key, Key West, Monroe County, Florida. *Library of Congress.*

Though the following story is not about the Key West Lighthouse, it is an exciting part of the area's history and takes place just off the island's shore in nearby Sand Key.

In the 1800s, Captain Joshua Appleby, a man from New England, moved to Key West, becoming the first white resident on the island. The captain supported himself by making money from what he found on shipwrecks off the shores of the Florida Keys.

There were a lot of questions about how he earned his money and his success. Many in the area believed he was a pirate searching for treasures at sea. Government officials noticed he was very good at finding treasure and eventually accused him of working with and conspiring with pirates to run ships aground so they could plunder the loot intentionally. However, the captain was released since they could not secure enough concrete evidence.

Then, out of the blue, the captain decided to make a surprising career shift. He started work as a lighthouse keeper of the Sand Key Lighthouse, just five miles off the shores of Key West, where he was in charge of protecting ships from disasters. No longer was he going to be making money off the unfortunate ships that tried to make their way to Key West.

After Appleby took charge of the lighthouse, the captain's daughter and her friends visited Sand Key Island in October 1846. Unfortunately, a devastating storm was heading right toward those visiting the island. This storm killed sixteen people, despite the fact they sought shelter in the nearby Sand Key Island lighthouse. During this storm, the entire lighthouse was washed away, leaving no trace of its existence or the visitors.

Though their bodies were never found, their spirits remained behind to haunt the small island.

The new lighthouse was built in 1853, and the new keepers claimed to hear the sounds of a voice believed to be the captain's and the voices of small children. In most cases, the voices were happy and content, but there were times when the voices sounded angry and agitated.

12

EGMONT KEY LIGHTHOUSE

ST. PETERSBURG, FLORIDA

I am a lighthouse, worn by the weather and the waves.
I keep my lamp lit to warn the sailors on their way.
—*"The Lighthouse's Tale," by Nickel Creek*

The history of Egmont Key and most of the Pinellas County area near Fort DeSoto dates back more than two thousand years; however, the first recorded landing on the small island was not until 1757, when Don Francisco Maria Celi, a Royal Spanish fleet pilot landed and named the island La Isla de San Blas y Barreda. Unfortunately, the name did not stick and was changed six years later when the Sunshine State became a British colony, and the island was named after the Second Earl of Egmont, John Pervecal.

Egmont Key was used as a detention area for Seminoles awaiting transfer during the Second Seminole War from 1835 to 1842. During this time, Seminoles were waiting to move west to the Indian Territory, now Oklahoma, and many did not survive their stay in the detention area.

It wasn't until 1848 that work on Egmont Key's first lighthouse was completed. Then, in September of the same year, a hurricane struck the island, covering it with six feet of water. The lighthouse keeper and his family endured the storm in a small boat tied to a tree. When the storm passed and the weather calmed down, the lighthouse keeper and his family rowed to Tampa, never to return to the lighthouse again.

Unfortunately, that year was not a good one for Egmont Key, and the area was struck by another hurricane only a few weeks later and again a few years later in 1852. The damage to the lighthouse was repaired, and the structure was rebuilt and restored in 1857; it was erected ninety feet farther inland to protect the tower better when facing threats of hurricanes. The Egmont Key Lighthouse was put back into service in 1858.

The Confederates removed the lighthouse lens during the Civil War to hinder the Union navy's efforts to set up a blockade of Tampa Bay. In July 1861, Egmont Key was captured by Union forces, and it served as a base for Union soldiers to attack Confederate ships in the waters of Tampa Bay. The island was also used as a military prison and a refuge for pro-Union sympathizers in Florida.

In 1864, a cemetery for Union and Confederate soldiers was opened on the island and maintained and managed until 1909. In 1909, the bodies in the cemetery were moved to other military cemeteries nationwide.

In preparation for the Spanish-American War, Fort Dade was built in 1898 on Egmont Key and was a base of operation to protect Tampa Bay from attacks by the Spanish navy. However, the Spanish fleet was destroyed in Cuba by the U.S. Navy and never made it to the Tampa Bay waters. Shortly after the event in Cuba, Spain surrendered and the war ended. Even though no battles, attacks or shots were fired on the island, it was used as a hospital where American soldiers returning from Cuba were quarantined.

The U.S. Fish and Wildlife Service took possession of the fort and turned the island over to the State of Florida. In 1989, the island was designated as a National Wildlife Refuge, and the Egmont Key State Park opened to the public.

Today, the 580-acre island has only remnants of buildings still standing on land and underwater, leaving about 300 acres available to explore above the water. The island has a grid of idyllic red brick streets, and heavy jungle vegetation has invaded the island. As a result, many people refer to the island as the Ghost Town of Egmont Key.

According to Greg Jenkins, author of *Florida's Ghostly Legends* and *Haunted Folklore: The Gulf Coast and Pensacola*, Egmont Key is home to at least one spirit spotted by one of the island's park rangers. This park ranger claims to encounter a man dressed in Civil War attire walking the island. Other paranormal encounters claim to see shadowy figures skulking around the lighthouse's base and a pale face peering out from the top of the tower.

So who are these spectral creatures lurking in the shadows of Egmont Key? Some say they are Seminole warriors, and others claim they are

Spanish explorers. There are also the spirits of Confederate and Union soldiers left behind after the war. And don't forget, there is always a possibility these shadow figures and apparitions are the spirits of former lighthouse keepers who continue to protect the island and perform their daily duties at the lighthouse.

13

CAPE SAN BLAS LIGHTHOUSE

PORT ST. JOE, FLORIDA

In the right light, at the right time, everything is extraordinary.
—Aaron Rose

Cape San Blas is located in the Florida Panhandle, near Destin, two hours from Tallahassee and an hour and a half from St. George Island. Four lighthouses have marked the southern portion of Cape San Blas, protecting the cape, which protrudes from the southernmost point of the Panhandle.

In 1847, permission was granted to build a lighthouse at the cape's elbow under the condition that the St. Joseph Bay Lighthouse was decommissioned and dismantled. The new lighthouse was completed in April 1848, but the Cape San Blas Lighthouse fell victim to a gale on August 23–24, 1851. This storm was the same storm that destroyed nearby lighthouses at Cape St. George and Dog Island.

About one year after losing the first lighthouse, Congress appropriated $12,000 to build a second brick lighthouse tower and keeper's dwelling for the cape. Unfortunately, the construction was hindered by an outbreak of yellow fever and delays in receiving the lantern and Fresnel lens. As a result, the new lighthouse tower and keeper's dwelling were not completed until November 1855, and Keeper Joseph Ridler transferred from Dog Island.

Just ten months later, on August 30, 1856, another devastating hurricane struck Cape San Blas, and the Lighthouse Board report about the storm stated, "The sea rose so high at that place that the waves struck the floor

Stereograph shows Cape San Blas Lighthouse with an attached house. *Library of Congress.*

of the keeper's dwelling, elevated eight feet above the ground, and about fourteen feet above the ordinary tides. A lagoon now occupies the site of that lighthouse."[13]

Following the devastation of another hurricane, Congress allocated $20,000 on March 3, 1857, to build a third brick tower and a two-story dwelling attached to the east side of the lighthouse. Then, at the outbreak of the Civil War, like many other lighthouses in Florida, the lens was removed from the Cape San Blas Lighthouse before Union forces could claim the area for themselves. During the Civil War, the keeper's dwelling and wooden parts of the lighthouse burned down.

On July 23, 1866, the lighthouse was returned to normal operations after a new lens was supplied and repairs to the damage from the war were completed, except for the keeper's residence. Unfortunately, Congress did not approve funds to rebuild the new dwelling until July 15, 1870, so until the new living quarters were completed, the keeper and their family were forced to live in the tower's small watch room.

Over the years, the front of the lighthouse disappeared, and by 1869, the Gulf waters were threatening the tower. The tower held its ground for as long as possible, but unfortunately, on July 3, 1882, it fell victim to the rising waters.

The following year, Congress granted funds to erect an iron skeleton tower fabricated in the North, and on its journey to the cape, the ship carrying the tower sank. Luckily, the structure landed in shallow water, and most of the material was salvaged. Work on the two lighthouse keeper dwellings and the lighthouse started in September 1884.

As the Gulf waters threatened the Cape Blas Lighthouse, Mother Nature struck again on October 8–9, 1894, when a mighty gale destroyed the keeper's residence and damaged the iron tower. The current lighthouse keeper, William Quinn, lost all his property, and the assistant keeper, George

L. Long, also suffered property losses during the storm. Finally, in 1904, as sand built up around the iron tower, it was decided by the Lighthouse Board to relocate the station and build two new keeper's dwellings.

The lighthouse tower was considered safe for many years until a hurricane in 1916 swept away the beach, protecting the lighthouse. Within one year of the storm and after continued beach erosion, the Cape San Blas Lighthouse tower stood about 120 feet offshore.

It was again decided the lighthouse would be moved, and it was temporarily put out of commission in 1918 as it was moved northward. When it was relocated, the lighthouse tower was set atop nine reinforced concrete blocks in January 1919.

The Cape San Blas Lighthouse faced many troubles, but it was not always a bowl full of cherries for the lighthouse keepers and their families. The station was isolated for decades, with the nearest settlement at least twenty-three miles away (one way).

The isolation was more than lighthouse keeper Ray Linton could handle. He found his duties overlooking operations at the lighthouse set on the vast expanse of the Gulf of Mexico a significant burden. In 1931, his duties had him rescuing two men and a girl in trouble while swimming off of the cape by fastening a gourd as a float to an end of the fishing line and securing the other end before wading into the waters to rescue the people swimming. Then, one lonely day in 1932, Linton took his own life.

Another tragic event occurred at the lighthouse when another keeper lost his life at the station six years later. Assistant keeper Ernest W. Marler was attacked and stabbed in a workshop at the lighthouse. He was thirty-eight years old and a father of four children. Unfortunately, his six-year-old daughter was the one who discovered his body when she went out to call him for the noon meal.

His murderer was never identified, but some claim it could have been local moonshiners or thieves he testified against a few days earlier.

Several years went by, and the dwellings at the lighthouse were left vacant. The lack of care and upkeep resulted in them deteriorating. The lighthouse was finally deactivated in 1996, and two years later, the lighthouse keeper's dwelling closest to the shore suffered immense damage from Hurricane Earl.

The Air Force assumed responsibility for the keeper's dwellings, and both structures were moved from their seat along the shore to a site next to the lighthouse tower in 1999. It was then that the residence in the best condition was restored, while the other dwelling had to wait until 2005 for its turn to be fully restored.

Mother Nature struck again, conjuring Hurricane Isaac to the Gulf Coast in August 2012, which again caused significant erosion at Cape San Blas. Now there was only a fifty-foot buffer between the keeper's dwellings and the waters of the Gulf. On October 14, 2012, operations at the lighthouse were shut down again, and the Air Force started preparations to move the tower and two dwellings. In early December of the same year, the two keeper's dwellings and the oil house were moved inland by about one hundred feet as a temporary measure.

The Air Force was anxious to offload the property, and in December 2012, the National Park Service was awarded ownership of the structures. At this time, an announcement was made about relocating the buildings to a public park and recreation area along the shore of St. Joseph Bay in nearby Port St. Joe. The official move of the lighthouse tower and the two dwellings occurred on July 15, 2014.

Locals claim the area surrounding the Cape San Blas Lighthouse in Port St. Joe is haunted. But are there experiences related to paranormal activity or the natural sounds of wild boars wailing in the distance? As you know, when it comes to the paranormal, anything is possible.

Additionally, some people have reported hearing footsteps in the upstairs hallway of the nearby Henry House Bay Side when no one else is home.

14

SEAHORSE LIGHTHOUSE

CEDAR KEY, FLORIDA

Aye, tales be plenty in this cursed place.
—*Pirates of the Caribbean, Walt Disney World*

Overlooking the channel to the Cedar Keys, set on an elevated area of Seahorse Key, there are three small rounded tombstones. These tombstones stand over the area like lonely sentinels, looking out, keeping watch and protecting the land. Each of these stones bears the name and references those buried there were associated with the U.S. Navy, which may hold the key to the paranormal activity reported throughout the island.

Concerning the U.S. Navy and the island's long connection to the military, there is an excellent chance that these three graves are for seamen who served their country and died on the island.

During the Second Seminole War, the island was used as the site of Cantonment Morgan, a U.S. military hospital and internment camp for Indians waiting to be relocated west. This site was abandoned in 1842, and the island was left for Mother Nature to regain control, providing an undisturbed sanctuary for native birds and wildlife.

In September 1851, by executive order of the president, Seahorse Key was reserved for lighthouse purposes. The 109 acres were declared property of the federal government, and all private claims to the island were invalidated.[14]

The first lighthouse keeper, William Wilson, took possession of the lighthouse, and the light was first illuminated on August 1, 1854. Wilson died in 1866 and was buried on the Seahorse Key, where he is believed to keep watch over the Cedar Keys and protect the nearby waterways.

Several years later, when the Civil War erupted in 1861, President Abraham Lincoln ordered naval ships to the Gulf Coast to create a blockade and seize vessels and cargoes to stop runners and halt salt-making efforts. When the Yankee navy took control in 1862, Seahorse Key and Depot Key were declared stopping points between Key West and St. Marks. During this time, the lighthouse was extinguished and relit on August 23, 1866.

Three young men went off to war and never thought when they left their homes and families it would be the last time they saw them. The first of the three navy seamen buried with the headstones at Seahorse Key was Ordinary Seaman Patrick Doran, born in Bushwick, New York, who first enlisted in the navy on November 20, 1861, in Philadelphia, Pennsylvania.

Doran served aboard USS *St. Louis*, USS *Keystone State*, USS *Princeton*, USS *Fort Henry* and USS *North Carolina* until he was killed in action on July 20, 1863, at the age of twenty-four in the engagement of the Waccasassa River. He was buried at Seahorse Key with customary ceremonies in the afternoon after he died in the engagement.

The second grave looking over Seahorse Key belongs to Ordinary Seaman Ephraim Hearn, born in Norfolk, Virginia, and enlisted in the navy in New York, New York, on March 29, 1862, for a three-year enlistment. During his time with the navy, he served aboard USS *North Carolina* and USS *Fort Henry*.

While serving aboard USS *Fort Henry*, on August 20, 1863, Hearn suffered from the bursting of a blood vessel and died at twenty-eight years old.

The third grave on Seahorse Key is that of Landsman William M. Robinson, born in Philadelphia, Pennsylvania, and enlisted in the navy on November 5, 1863, for a one-year term. Robinson served aboard USS *North Carolina*, USS *Union* and USS *Neptune*. While serving aboard USS *Union*, Robinson died on March 14, 1864, due to brain compression he suffered from a fall at twenty-three years of age.

Today, the graves sit on the island, which is only accessible by boat, and are surrounded by the many birds that call the island home. As part of the Cedar Keys National Wildlife Refuge, Seahorse Key is one of Florida's most significant bird nesting areas. Still, it is also home to many spirits lurking in the shadows, including the spirits of the three men buried on the island.

Before the Civil War took the attention of many in the Cedar Key area, the Second Seminole Indian War caused much devastation to the site, including Seahorse Key. During this war, the U.S. military occupied Cedar Key, using it as a supply depot and hospital. At the same time, Seahorse Key remained a detention camp for Indians waiting to be relocated out west.

General Zachary Taylor requested that the Cedar Keys be reserved for military use. It was already determined during this conflict that it would be the site of a lighthouse sometime in the future. When Taylor became president in 1849, he had the authority to make his dream of a lighthouse on Seahorse Key come true. However, he died a little more than one year after taking office, in September 1850, so he could not see his prophecy fulfilled.

Congress authorized the use of $8,000 to erect the lighthouse President Taylor wanted to sit on the shores of Seahorse Key. Finally, on September 2, 1851, orders for the lighthouse were approved, and the following year, another $4,000 was set aside to erect the lighthouse.

Once completed, the lighthouse tower was accompanied by a seventy-square-foot dwelling with a spiral staircase leading up to the top of the lighthouse. The wicks for the tower's Fresnel lens were lit by the lighthouse keeper, William Wilson, on August 1, 1854. The light from the lighthouse was visible up to fifteen miles from Seahorse Key.

The lighthouse on Seahorse Key did more than just alert ships. They were coming close to shore. Soon, the Cedar Keys started to attract commercial enterprises seeking to access the area's plentiful cedar trees to manufacture pencils and other goods. Eberhard Faber purchased large tracts of land on the islands in 1855 and opened a pencil mill on Atsena Otie Key.

Though the Cedar Keys were prosperous during the years following the war, businesses suffered when a hurricane struck the keys in 1896, destroying many of the factories and mills in the area. This was just one of many traumatic incidents the island area suffered that could be a source of the paranormal activity on Seahorse Key.[15]

One of the scariest paranormal experiences reported in Cedar Key near the Seahorse Lighthouse is that of a headless pirate riding a palomino believed to haunt the area at night. Many believe this headless apparition is the spirit of Pierre LeBlanc, a pirate known for working for the notorious Jean Lafitte.

Lafitte left LeBlanc behind with a palomino and some supplies, putting LeBlanc in charge of guarding the buried treasure on Seahorse Key. However, a stranger spotted LeBlanc and built a friendship, which finally led LeBlanc to reveal the treasure's location. Then one night, when LeBlanc had too much to drink and passed out, the stranger took advantage of knowing where the treasure was and claimed the booty.

When LeBlanc woke up, he attacked the stranger but lost the fight, resulting in the loss of his head.

Additionally, on Cedar Key, there is a shell mound created by local Native Americans more than one thousand years ago that is now included in the Lower Suwannee National Wildlife Refuge. A nature trail encompasses the mound called Shell Mound Trail, and many explorers have encountered spirits from the past.

Many locals believe the area to be extremely haunted, particularly the site where the ghost of Annie Simpson and her dog are believed to roam. So who was Annie Simpson, and why would her spirit and the spirit of her canine companion haunt the island? Let's take a closer look.

Local legend shares a story about pirates from long ago who buried a treasure in Cedar Key. When Simpson and her wolfhound accidentally stumbled across the treasure's location, the pirates killed the two in an attempt to keep their location a secret.

Paranormal claims related to witnessing the spirit of Simpson and her dog include seeing a white glowing light floating in the area where she was believed to have been killed. Others claim to see a body in a white dress, but no arms or legs, floating around in the air, and others claim to see her full-bodied apparition.

As the years passed, several reports of a ghostly vision drifting through the woods near the Shell Mound Trail were spotted by local fishermen. The spirit appeared to be a beautiful young girl wearing a pale blouse and a long dark skirt. The young girl's spirit is often spotted standing near the edge of the woods with her hand resting on the head of her giant shaggy hound.

Some fishermen claim she would silently outstretch her hand toward them as if she was calling them to follow her. Others have claimed she would fade away into a soft white mist.

Upon further exploration of the island, treasure hunters have claimed to unearth small caches of coins and even discovered an intact skeleton of a very large dog. However, Simpson's body was never found, which could be why her spirit wanders in the woods, waiting for someone to discover her body and take her home.

The hiking trail around Shell Mount is sparsely inhabited, but many native birds live and nest in the trees filling the island. The woods surrounding the mound have oaks covered in old stately moss, and the nearby swamp blooms with spring wildflowers, which add to the eeriness of the Cedar Keys and the area surrounding the Seahorse Key Lighthouse.

Other paranormal encounters include hearing the sounds of hoofs thundering down the beach, with no trace of horses or anything else that could be responsible for creating the sounds.

Inside the lighthouse, several people claimed to have heard footsteps in the tower's stairwell and a muffled voice whispering from below.

Another grave lies on Seahorse Key, that of Joseph Napoleon Crevasse, who died in 1874 and now lies among the palmettos and palms. He was once a ship's captain and a Civil War blockade runner and is believed to still wander among the trees peering out at the open sea.

The sad, bloody history of Seahorse Key has led to the manifestation of shadows and spectral figures sticking around from the island's tragic past.

15

GARDEN KEY LIGHTHOUSE

TORTUGAS HARBOR
KEY WEST, FLORIDA

There is a special place, at the end of nowhere, but on the way to everywhere, a place of explorers, pirates, smugglers, soldiers, prisoners and scientists. This is a place where some men lost hope, and many died in despair.
—*L. Wayne Landrum*

G arden Key Lighthouse is set in Fort Jefferson in the Dry Tortugas National Park off the shores of Key West, Florida, and like many lighthouse locations throughout the area, it is home to many ghosts and legends. Tortugas Harbor is a beautiful location surrounded by crystal clear waters, full of hidden gems and just a stone's throw from Key West.

When visiting Fort Jefferson, it is hard to believe the island is full of paranormal activity because of the beautiful beaches found along the waters near the lighthouse. But the historical past is what fuels the paranormal activity. It keeps a hold on the past, often bringing it into the present for anyone to see and experience it.

The island's recorded history started when the Spanish explorer Ponce de Leon bestowed the Dry Tortugas their name in 1513, the second-oldest European name on record in the United States. The Tortugas, "turtles" in Spanish, were home to an immense population of sea turtles that called the inlets their home. The word *Dry* was added later and served as a way to tell mariners that the islands were lacking freshwater sources.

The crew from HMS *Tyger* were shipwrecked on Garden Key in the Dry Tortugas in 1742 for more than fifty-six days. While struggling to survive

Fort Jefferson Lighthouse. *Library of Congress, Dale M. McDonald.*

in the desolate landscape, they fought off a Spanish sloop and eventually saved their lives by constructing improvised boats out of the few supplies they could find on the island and sailing their way to Jamaica.

Several exciting things occurred on and around Garden Key, giving the Dry Tortugas the unique history for which the area is known.

A 1622 Spanish treasure fleet containing copper, gold, silver, glass, olive jars and other artifacts was believed to have sunk off the shores of the Florida Keys. The Seahawk Deep Ocean Technology examined a wreck in 1989 believed to have been a part of this treasure fleet.

One ship from the Spanish treasure fleet suffered damage from being battered by a hurricane on September 6, 1622, and was driven head-first onto a coral reef. The *Nuestra Señora de Atocha* was discovered on July 20, 1985, by Mel Fisher and his organization, and they uncovered more than $450 million in gold, silver and other valuable artifacts. The ship was dubbed "The Atocha Motherlode," and Fisher became well known for finding this shipwreck, as well as others in the waters off of Florida, including *Atocha*'s sister ship, the *Santa Margarita*.

Fort Jefferson was the site of a historic prison that housed famous prisoners and served as a fort during the Civil War. The fortress on this lonely island housed many prisoners throughout the years, including Dr. Samuel Mudd, who was involved in the assassination of President Abraham Lincoln.

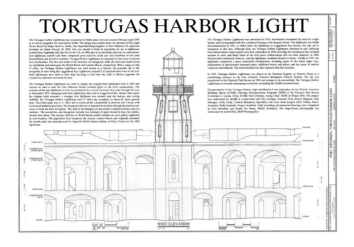

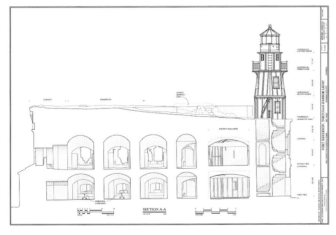

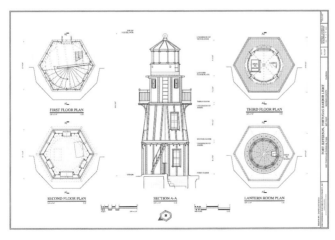

Top: Cover Sheet, West Elevation—Fort Jefferson, Tortugas Harbor Light, Garden Key, Key West, Monroe County, Florida. Drawings from Survey HABS FL-44-F. *Library of Congress.*

Middle: Longitudinal Section—Fort Jefferson, Tortugas Harbor Light, Garden Key, Key West, Monroe County, Florida. Drawings from Survey HABS FL-44-F. *Library of Congress.*

Bottom: Section and Plans—Fort Jefferson, Tortugas Harbor Light, Garden Key, Key West, Monroe County, Florida. Drawings from Survey HABS FL-44-F. *Library of Congress.*

With more than sixteen million bricks, this bulky coastal fortress is the largest brick masonry structure in the United States. Despite never being finished, it is the main historical attraction of the Dry Tortugas National Park.

Throughout the years, the fort served as a strategic point in the Caribbean and was instrumental in defending the area against ruffians, privateers and pirates. During the Civil War, Fort Jefferson remained in Union control and was where they kept watching over Confederate movements in the Gulf of Mexico. However, when the war ended, the island became a prison.

Tragic event after tragic event hit Garden Key, such as vandals, hurricanes, yellow fever epidemics and an army garrison that operated and administered the fort but was rumored to have a screw loose (or two). At one point in the island's history, it served as a Marine Hospital Service site for quarantine and coal distribution to the U.S. Navy ships. In the end, a small caretaker force was put in charge of the fort.

Legend claims the island even suffered more horrific events, such as cannibalism, murder, executions, drownings, prison fights and the outbreak of other diseases. All of these tragic events provide fuel for paranormal activity and could be the explanation as to who haunts Garden Key and why.

Visitors and workers on Garden Key and at Fort Jefferson claim the island is riddled with supernatural phenomena, including wild poltergeists, specters, shadow people and much more. Many rangers have returned home with chilling stories to share with friends and family about the strange occurrences experienced during their duties on the island.

The hallways of Fort Jefferson have an eerie feeling, and sensitives can feel unusual energies emanating from the walls. Sounds of what many believe to be the devil himself howl through the air at midnight. Strange lights have appeared in the sky, hovering over the waters offshore from Fort Jefferson. Many lucky enough to camp on the island typically return home, never to visit Garden Key again.

It is believed that the actions of prison guards and the military during and after the Civil War significantly contributed to the many paranormal accounts on Garden Key. For example, when Dr. Mudd was a prisoner on the island, he witnessed havoc, pandemonium and many people dying from yellow fever, which ran rampant in Fort Jefferson. It seemed as if the military was tossing the victims of this pandemic into the sea daily.

Dr. Mudd sprang into action, helping nurses and military personnel treat and prevent the spread of yellow fever. Guards wrote a letter to President Jackson about Dr. Mudd's heroic efforts at Fort Jefferson, and he, along with two other assassination conspirators, was pardoned.

Some believe Dr. Mudd's spirit and yellow fever victims still haunt the fort's halls. Many claim the apparitions and sounds of moaning are those of the pandemic's victims. They could also be Dr. Mudd and the nursing staff frantically working to save as many prisoners as possible.

It is safe to say that horrific events of the past haunt Garden Key in the Dry Tortugas National Park, and many people who once lived, worked or were imprisoned on the island remain behind today.

16

CROOKED RIVER LIGHTHOUSE

CARRABELLE, FLORIDA

The dip of the light meant that the island itself was always left in darkness.
A lighthouse is for others; powerless to illuminate the space closest to it.
—*M.L. Stedman*

Initially built in 1895, the historic Crooked River Lighthouse was listed on the National Register of Historic Places and was restored in 2007. Unlike the more popular Florida lighthouses, the Crooked River Lighthouse is one of several iron skeleton structures topped with a circular parapet to shed light on the sea to guide sailors back to shore.

This lighthouse has 128 steps that wind up to the top of the 103-foot-tall lighthouse, the largest on the Forgotten Coast.[16] Today, the Keeper's House Museum houses the lighthouse's original fourth-order Fresnel lens constructed in Paris, France, in 1894. The museum also houses several artifacts from the area, including the lighthouse's original clock, an antique glass fire grenade, pages from the lighthouse keeper's watch book, jewelry and more. These items are believed to hold the energies of many spirits belonging to those who once called the lighthouse area home.

There are few paranormal reports associated with the Crooked River Lighthouse. Still, some claims are found online that share stories of seeing shadow people walking along the base of the lighthouse, strange noises in the museum and a sensation of being watched.

17

SANIBEL ISLAND LIGHTHOUSE

SANIBEL, FLORIDA

A lighthouse doesn't save the ships; it doesn't go out and rescue them,
it's just this pillar that helps to guide people home.
—Lea Michele

Southwest Florida is littered with barrier islands of all shapes and sizes. Sanibel Island is a slender, crescent-shaped island most known for the abundance of seashells visitors can gather. Though numerous shell collectors flock to the island, the Sanibel Island Lighthouse is another famous site for tourists and visitors.

Sanibel Island was only accessible by ferry until the canal between the mainland and the island was constructed in 1963. Notable visitors to the island include Henry Ford and Thomas Edison. Still, a small settlement was established on the island in 1833, and the residents petitioned to construct a lighthouse. Unfortunately, this petition failed, and eventually, the tiny settlement fell due to disease and other hardships, leaving the island abandoned within less than five years of their arrival.

Funding requests for a lighthouse to be built on Sanibel Island were rejected in 1856 and again after the Civil War in 1878. Finally, Congress granted funds to be used in the erection of a lighthouse in 1883, and work began on the eastern tip of the island in February 1884. Much of the lighthouse was constructed on the island. Still, the ironwork needed for the lighthouse was transported to the island by sea. The ship carrying the ironwork from Jersey City for Sanibel Island and Cape San Blas sank about two miles off Sanibel Island.

The Sanibel
Lighthouse on
Sanibel Island, an
island and small
city south of Fort
Myers, on Florida's
southwest coast on
the Gulf of Mexico,
has guided ships
into the entrance
to San Carlos Bay.
*Library of Congress,
Carol M. Highsmith.*

Crews aboard the vessel and a diver were able to pull up all the pieces, getting them ready to construct the lighthouse. Finally, the lighthouse was ready to be lit on August 20, 1884, and the first lighthouse keeper on the island, Dudley Richardson, lit the lighthouse, illuminating the shores surrounding Sanibel Island.

In 1888, Henry Shanahan, with his wife and two sons, moved to the island and eventually became the assistant lighthouse keeper. Then, when Richardson resigned in 1892, Shanahan applied for the position of head lighthouse keeper, which was initially refused because he was illiterate; however, when he threatened to otherwise resign from his current role, they gave him the promotion.

Sadly, a few years later, Shanahan's wife died, leaving him alone to care for their seven children until he met the widow Irene Rutland, who was living on the island raising her five children. The two married and had another son together, and the family of thirteen children helped run the Sanibel Lighthouse.

Shanahan died after twenty-three years of service at the lighthouse in 1913, and his son, who served as the assistant lighthouse keeper, returned in 1924 to continue his father's legacy of taking care of the lighthouse. In the 1920s and again in the 1930s, one of Shanahan's stepsons served as the assistant lighthouse keeper.

Another death occurred on the island associated with the Sanibel Island Lighthouse when assistant lighthouse keeper Richard T. Barry was murdered by Jesse W. Lee on June 26, 1919. It was rumored that Barry had insulted

A mid-island canal on Sanibel Island, an island and small city south of Fort Myers, on Florida's southwest coast on the Gulf of Mexico. *Library of Congress, Carol M. Highsmith.*

Lee's wife, creating the motive for the murder. Lee admitted to killing the assistant lighthouse keeper but claimed it was in self-defense, resulting in his being acquitted of the murder.

After Coastguardsman Bob England and his wife, Mae, and infant daughter Margaret came to the island to operate the lighthouse in 1946, it was struck by a hurricane and suffered severe erosion one year later. Due to concerns about erosion on the island and that one of the dwellings was left standing in a foot of water, it was decided that the lighthouse would be automated and assigned to the Fort Myers Coast Guard Station for monitoring. From this station, England continued to service the Sanibel Island Lighthouse, providing navigation aids to the area.

Several changes occurred to the lighthouse throughout the years, including becoming electrified in 1962 by the Coast Guard. Then in 1972, the Coast Guard proposed the lighthouse be decommissioned, but local residents and mariners convinced the City of Sanibel to assume management of the property. In 2000, the property was officially transferred from the Coast Guard to the Bureau of Land Management. After a lengthy delay, the lighthouse was formally transferred to the city, and a ceremony was held on April 21, 2010.[17]

No one really knows what haunts the Sanibel Island Lighthouse, the keeper's dwellings or the surrounding areas. Though the island has suffered some tragic events, the trauma that affected the site is not as severe as some other Florida lighthouses have suffered. Very few reports of paranormal activity exist about hauntings and spirits hanging out at the lighthouse.

Long view of the fishing pier on Sanibel Island, an island and small city south of Fort Myers, on Florida's southwest coast on the Gulf of Mexico. *Library of Congress, Carol M. Highsmith.*

Still, some paranormal researchers have shared stories about shadow figures, eerie noises, footsteps, cold spots and strange light anomalies in the lighthouse and throughout the property.

There is always a chance the Sanibel Island Lighthouse is haunted, and with little information available, it provides many opportunities to research, explore, investigate and discover.

18

AMELIA ISLAND LIGHTHOUSE

FERNANDINA BEACH, FLORIDA

Lighthouses are not just stone, brick, metal and glass.
There's a human story at every lighthouse; that's the story I want to tell.
—*Elinor DeWire*

Florida is home to several historical structures, but none boast the same heritage or longevity as the Amelia Island Lighthouse. Built in 1838, the Amelia Island Lighthouse is the state's oldest lighthouse and the only one remaining from the territorial period without any significant major repairs, rebuilding or relocation.[18]

Florida was not yet a state when the light first shone from the lighthouse tower. Nevertheless, the light beacon has been kept shining, guiding freighters, fishing boats and seafarers into the channel toward the Fernandina Harbor.

The Coast Guard handed over possession of the lighthouse in 2001 to the City of Fernandina Beach, and the city has preserved the monument as one of the island's most visible and beloved historic sites. The town maintained the property, while the Coast Guard, with the assistance of local Coast Guard Auxiliary volunteers, worked to maintain and keep the light beacon functional.

The history of Amelia Island is full of stories about pirates, bootleggers and other nefarious individuals. With many reports of paranormal activity throughout the area, there is no wonder if the lighthouse is haunted, casting a spooky image across the coast. As it is the oldest working lighthouse in Florida, visitors and workers have heard everything from eerie voices to footsteps following them up the tower and shadow figures to full-bodied apparitions within the lighthouse and throughout the property.

Some of Amelia Island Lighthouse's paranormal activity can also be explained by the many traumatic events and paranormal accounts within one to two miles of the lighthouse property.

One of the most haunted locations on the island is about two miles away to the west of the Amelia Island Lighthouse. The Nassau County Jailhouse is the current location for Florida's first spoken-word museum, where the infamous pirate Louis-Michel Aury was jailed the night before his execution.

Aury arrived in Fernandina in 1817, intending to take over the island by raising the Mexican Republic flag over the area. Instead, he was captured, tried and sentenced to hang for his many horrific crimes. In an attempt to avoid any humiliation associated with being executed by the hangman's noose, Aury slit his own throat the night before his execution. However, his attempts did not succeed the way he had hoped, and he was caught trying to slit his throat, and the jailhouse surgeon kept him alive by crudely stitching up his wound.

Aury was not allowed recovery time after his botched suicide attempt and quick yet patchy surgery, and he was sent to the gallows the next day out behind the jailhouse.

Locals have had several encounters with the ghost of Aury, and he seems to be more active around the jailhouse. Several people have heard sounds of moaning around the jail, and some have seen the apparition of a bloody pirate with a gash in his neck. It is believed this apparition is that of Aury.

Another haunted location on Amelia Island is the Williams House, one of the oldest and most historic homes in the Fernandina Beach area. This home is about two miles from the lighthouse and was purchased in 1858 by Marcellus A. Williams, who fled from the house when Union troops occupied their home during the Civil War.

When Williams returned to his home after releasing his slaves, he became an active part of the Underground Railroad, offering his home on Amelia Island as a safe house for runaway slaves. Inside the home is a hidden room near the dining room where slaves hid inside until it was safe to travel.

The antebellum mansion has many reports of paranormal activity, which could be tied to the fun and excitement in the home before the Civil War but could also be connected to the activities associated with the Underground Railroad.

Several visitors have heard laughter, glasses clinking, friendly chatter and other sounds of partying guests in the dining room. In addition, some visitors have seen apparitions descending the staircase, including a female ghost who stops at the mirror near the stairs. This female apparition is also seen appearing now and then in the same mirror but as a reflection instead of a full-bodied apparition.

Two more apparitions, a man and a woman, are spotted near the stairs of the Williams House, and when the living make eye contact with these spectral guests, they suddenly disappear. Many of the ghosts at the Williams House appear happy, friendly and nonthreatening.

Set less than two miles from the lighthouse was the Florida House Inn, which provided views of the lighthouse for the railroad employees who lived in the structure built in 1857. The home was also used to house Union officers during the Civil War, including Major Leddy, who bought the house after the war and ran the hotel with his wife. It appears as if "Miz Leddy," the major's wife, still hangs around the house because it is her favorite place to be. Bartenders at the Inn have caught the scent of her strong lavender perfume and spotted antique shoes going missing from their display near the desk, only to be found later in a guest's room.

Though not all cemeteries are haunted, one is about two miles from the Amelia Island Lighthouse to the northwest, surrounded by large trees with hanging moss and nicknamed "Beautiful Woods." The Bosque Bello Cemetery is stunningly beautiful and is one of the oldest in the state of Florida, with graves of Amelia Island Lighthouse keepers, nineteenth-century Spanish residents, gun runners, boat captains, politicians, magicians, nuns, veterans from many wars and victims of yellow and typhoid fever epidemics.

Visitors and paranormal researchers who have investigated the Bosque Bello Cemetery have reported hearing disembodied voices and laughter, which get louder as the sun sets on the cemetery. In addition, spirits and entities in the form of children have appeared, wandering among the tombstones. Some have been spotted sitting high in the treetops monitoring visitors' every move.

Egan's Creek Greenway is less than two miles from the Amelia Island Lighthouse, where three hundred acres of marsh landscape are protected today. Still, it was once the location of extensive pirate activity in the area. The world was different in 1900, and Florida was the site of heavy pirate activity, especially among those looking to buy substantial amounts of treasure in desolate areas.

Once the treasure was buried, pirates would kill their accomplices, leaving their bodies and souls to haunt the island, looking for their killer.

One local legend related to a buried treasure in the area of Egan's Creek Greenway is of one pirate who did everything possible to cover his tracks by killing his accomplices and leaving a chain over the limb of a giant oak tree as his version of the *X* marks the spot. However, no matter how carefully he protected his buried treasure, a rattlesnake bit him, and he lay there under the tree as his final resting place.

Locals share stories that if you are hiking at Egan's Creek and see the rusty chain swinging from an old oak tree, you are to leave the "money tree" alone or risk upsetting the spirit of the pirate.

One final legend associated with paranormal activity within less than one mile of the Amelia Island Lighthouse is at Fort Clinch State Park. This park houses one of the most well-preserved nineteenth-century forts in the United States, and though it was garrisoned during the Civil War and the Spanish-American War, this fort never saw any battle.

Preservation of the old abandoned fort finally began in the 1930s, and it was admitted to the state park system in 1935. Several ghostly tales have been passed down through the decades, including the legend of a Civil War soldier believed to have been stationed at Fort Clinch who wrote his beloved a letter in which he promised not to die until he had the opportunity to see her one more time. Sadly, he could not fulfill this promise, as he died during a Confederate ambush of the fort.

Legend claims his angry ghost roams the fort and quietly walks the fort grounds at dusk. It is believed that if someone sees a Confederate soldier walking the park grounds, it is best to turn the other way and find a different walking path to avoid the angry, evil spirit.

19

ANCLOTE KEY LIGHTHOUSE

TARPON SPRINGS, FLORIDA

Once the lighthouse is seen, the rest of the sea is ignored.
—*Terri Guillemets*

Anclote Key is a beautiful area in West Central Florida with a rich history of days gone by. The site and surrounding waterways were ideal for supporting Indigenous Indians, explorers, pirates and pioneers. Though these people created a life in Anclote Key's historical past, several ghosts today occupy the area's shores, especially around the lighthouse.

The lighthouse is set in Anclote Key Preserve State Park, which was the location where Timucuan Indians would migrate to during times of the year when fish and shellfish were plentiful in the waters just offshore. Then, during winter, they would move inland to hunt deer, bear, alligator and other wild game.

In the 1500s, Alonso Álvarez de Pineda and Vasco da Gama, two great Spanish explorers, came to the area with their conquistadors to start surveying the area. The site was named after the anchors used to pull the ships forward to reach their destination and help them navigate the shallow, winding channels between them and the land. The word *anclote* translates to "anchor," which explains the naming of the Anclote community, Anclote Key and Anclote River.

The Spanish galleons were full of treasures and supplies, and many of them fell victim to buccaneers and pirates who lay in wait to attack and loot the vessels as they roamed along the waters off the Anclote area. Once the loot was captured, the pirates were believed to have buried their booty nearby.

Hostilities arose between the Spanish explorers and the Timucuans over a freshwater source a few yards from the riverbanks. The Timucuans discovered this source, which they called "sweet water," and it was later known as the Spanish Well. Unfortunately, many died on both sides of the feud, and the Timucua tribes were subsequently wiped out by diseases carried by Europeans as they came to explore new lands. As a result, in the end, control of this water source landed in the hands of the Spanish explorers.

Florida played an instrumental role during the Civil War by providing cattle to the Confederate army. Anclote Key was used as a staging area in preparation for an attempted attack on the city of Brooksville. Brooksville is where the cattle were raised and housed until needed by the Confederate soldiers.

Additionally, south of the Anclote River is an area known as Deserter's Hill. Legend has it that Confederate deserters escaped to this hill before trying to swim out to the federal gunships just off the shores of Anclote Key. Unfortunately, the soldiers were captured en route to the ships and put to death for deserting their military post.

It is believed that one of these soldiers could be the spirit named Jacks, who appears to be from the Civil War era and haunts the women of the community, especially those visiting the lighthouse. This spirit has also been spotted atop Deserter's Hill and other surrounding areas.

In 1887, the Anclote Key Lighthouse was built, and construction took a short time, mainly because most of the structure was prefabricated in another location. After three months of construction, the cast-iron lighthouse tower was finally lit by Keeper James Gardner on September 15, 1887. The lighthouse is still in working order, illuminating the crystal-clear waters at night, where some people have discovered gold coins and submerged treasures while scuba diving in the nearby waters.

On October 6, 1889, according to the keeper's log, the keeper and his wife's baby fell ill, and the baby boy died the following morning. The keeper and his wife buried the baby on the island the same day. The baby's death could be the key to unlocking some of the paranormal activity, but it is still uncertain who or what really haunts the lighthouse property.

There are several reports of pirates searching the shores of Anclote Key for their buried treasure and scaring away anyone who may have gotten too close to where their loot is buried. Many visitors to Anclote Key and the lighthouse hear strange voices, see apparitions and are encountered by various unexplainable entities. Yet outside of the Confederate soldier who haunts the key, it is uncertain who exactly remains behind, making their presence known to those who visit.

20

St. Johns River Lighthouse

Jacksonville, Florida

I am haunted by waters.
—Norman Maclean

The St. Johns River winds through more than three hundred miles of wetlands, cypress forests and swamps in the wilds of Florida and is the longest and widest river in the Sunshine State. The river is known for being relatively slow, providing a lazy flow northward instead of the typical southward-flowing river.

Though the waters of the St. Johns River and attached lakes are famous among outdoor and water-sports recreation enthusiasts, there is a dark history of strange creatures hiding on the shores and within the river's murky waters.

One legend most commonly shared when discussing strange occurrences along the St. Johns River is that of the St. Johns Monster, which appeared in local folklore in the 1950s. Many have tried to say that the monster was a dolphin or manatee, but some have described the creature that stalks the muddy depths of the river as more of a prehistoric dinosaur. Descriptions of this creature depict a bipedal sauropod, a reptilian beast or a shapeless blob.

Though the descriptions of the monster are inconsistent, the fact that there is a monster seen at various points along the river, including near the St. Johns River Lighthouse, leads many to believe in the possibility of something cryptid lying beneath the surface of the river's water.

The creepiness of the creature that lurks in the water of the St. Johns River adds to the haunted feeling when visiting the St. Johns River Lighthouse.

The first lighthouse in the area was constructed in 1830, but it did not stand long before suffering from the impact of storm surges, which weakened the base of the structure.

The old tower was torn down in 1835, and a new one was built, but the new one was located a little bit farther up the river's shoreline from the site of the original tower. Unfortunately, the second lighthouse tower was not strong enough to last. In the 1850s, it was deemed unusable because excessive amounts of sand collected along the dune line by the tower, which caused a blockage, making the light challenging for mariners to see. Because of this, the lighthouse was deemed useless, and a third lighthouse had to be built.

The third tower was only sixty feet tall and equipped with a third-order Fresnel lens, and following the Civil War, the tower was raised, bringing it to its current height of eighty-one feet.

In an attempt to avoid the fate of the St. Johns River Light's predecessors, the lighthouse tower was constructed substantially taller than the previous two and farther inland away from the waterline. Unfortunately, as with many lighthouses in Florida, during the Civil War, the St. Johns River Lighthouse was extinguished to protect the shores from Union invasion.

The lighthouse keeper at the time, John Daniels, remained at the lighthouse, maintaining and protecting the property. However, he was arrested when federal forces occupied the area for sending light signals to Confederate regiments from the tower during the dark of night.

The story about Daniels is just one of many tied to the lighthouses constructed along the St. Johns River.

Another legend, as described by Wanton S. Webb,[19] shares the story of "a pretty romance." This story is about a retired maritime sergeant known to have locked his daughter in the Hazard Light, the name for the lighthouse at the mouth of the St. Johns River. Unfortunately, there are no exact dates when this event occurred and not many specific details. Still, the legend claims that Sergeant Brandt's daughter, Fanny, had become popular among the captains, lieutenants and officers of every rank at the nearby naval arsenal. All of them were attempting to court Fanny.

One day a young officer compromised the sergeant's daughter's honor, and when she became pregnant, the old sergeant was concerned with the scandal that would follow the incident. Eventually, the sergeant and his daughter disappeared, and only a few knew where they had gone. The two had left the area and were left on the steps of the Hazard Light as the new lighthouse keeper.

Legend claims the sergeant wanted his daughter to suffer a long spell of repentance, and she was imprisoned in the tower. From her window, she witnessed her father take the young officer out in a boat to sea. Fearing the worst, she worried about the safety of her beloved, but he returned and waited for her to complete the sentence her father gave her.

After fully repenting, the young officer made Fanny his bride, with the full support of the sergeant. There is no mention of what happened with the sergeant, his daughter, the young officer or their baby after she was released from her prison sentence and the couple married.

Throughout the years, the lighthouse was eroded by the constant exposure to salt air and battering from the surf, but the copper roof of the lighthouse remained steady, sound and robust. There have been updates and renovations completed to help keep it looking good and functioning correctly. In addition, the light and the enclosure were also dismantled, repaired and replaced.

Today, the inside of the Old St. Johns Lighthouse is dark, humid and musty smelling. It almost feels like stepping through a portal into another time or dimension while climbing up or down the spiral stairwell. Climbing this stairwell is not for those who are afraid of tight spaces because the spiral is tightly wound and feels constricted.

It is easy to envision climbing the stairs to the prison where Fanny spent her pregnancy before marrying her true love. Even if this lighthouse was not the lighthouse mentioned in the legend (because there is no date), it is still an eerie feeling to ascend these stairs with the knowledge of the legend.

Though the St. Johns River Lighthouse was decommissioned in 1929, it still stands near the mouth of the river on the grounds of the naval station in the Mayport area. After seventy years of service, the Old St. Johns River Lighthouse was replaced by the St. Johns Lightship (LV-84), which moored about eight miles offshore across the river's mouth.

Today, the Old St. Johns River Lighthouse is listed on the National Register of Historic Places (since 1976) and is the oldest surviving structure in Mayport. The red brick tower, slate stairs and balcony are available for public viewing and exploring.

With many exciting and tragic stories at the three different lighthouses, there is no doubt the waters of the St. Johns River are haunted. Many who have visited the newest of the three tower structures report hearing strange noises in the cramped stairwell, sounds of footsteps and the sensation of someone watching from the shadows. Others have reported seeing apparitions on the beach and the grounds surrounding the three lighthouse properties.

21

SAND KEY LIGHTHOUSE

KEY WEST, FLORIDA

There's a part of me that thinks perhaps we go on existing in a place
even after we've left it.
—Colum McCann

The paranormal activity associated with the Key West Lighthouse has been previously discussed and a brief mention of the nearby Sand Key Lighthouse introduced. Continue reading to learn more about the history and hauntings surrounding the lighthouse set close to one of the most haunted structures in Florida.

The Havana Hurricane that rolled through the area in 1846 killed at least sixty people in the Key West area, and many of their spirits are believed to haunt the island and the surrounding waters. Both lighthouses in Key West, the Key West Lighthouse and the Sand Key Lighthouse, are haunted by apparitions, supernatural activity and disembodied voices, many believed to be the victims of the Havana Hurricane.

The Sand Key Lighthouse is set far offshore and is the most notable lighthouse in the Florida Keys. This lighthouse warns ships about the dangerous Florida Reef below the surface of the water, where many Spanish galleons were lost traveling through the waters of the Gulf Stream in the 1500s.

The Florida Reef stretched along the surf off the Florida Keys against the edge of the deep water. The keel-crunching reef lay invisible under the water's surface, and even under suitable conditions, the most skilled mariners

North Corner—Sand Key Lighthouse, Sand Key, Key West, Monroe County, Florida. *Library of Congress.*

would stray onto it. Unfortunately, stormy weather made navigating the waters more challenging, and several ships could barely make their way through the area—some were washed aground on the reef.

Many ships that crashed into the reef met their final resting place at the bottom of the deep ocean water just off the reef's shelf. At the same time, other ships could be rescued by the wreckers who worked the area salvaging and saving stranded vessels on the reef.

In addition to the Florida Reef being an enemy of many mariners, pirates flooded the area, unlawfully capturing ships in the waters surrounding the Florida Keys. The pirates would steal the cargo and vessels, and in several cases, the more menacing pirates were known for murdering the entire crew, leaving no one behind.

Unlike the pirates, wreckers were not in it for the money. Instead, local courts set up rules to adjudicate wrecker activity, and all boats used for this service had to be licensed.

However, some wreckers were not honest in their endeavors off the shores of Key West. Stories abound about wreckers who set up false navigation lights to confuse ship captains in an attempt to lead them onto

 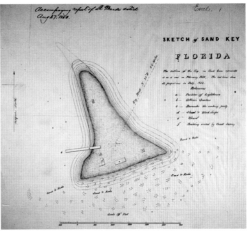

Left: Sand Key Lighthouse, Sand Key, Key West, Monroe County, Florida. *Library of Congress.*

Right: Photocopy of topographical drawing (from National Archives) Delineator unknown, dated August 27, 1853 "SKETCH OF SAND KEY FLORIDA"—Sand Key Lighthouse, Sand Key, Key West, Monroe County. *Library of Congress.*

the reef. Then they would come to the rescue and often charge fees to pull the ship to safety. This practice of wrecking was made illegal in Key West, and thanks to the 1823 law, it was punishable by death.

In an effort to protect the ships navigating the waters near the Florida Reef, a series of lighthouses were installed off the shores closer to the reef. Finally, in 1827 the Sand Key Lighthouse was constructed, but the first tower, like the Key West Lighthouse, fell victim to the 1846 Havana Hurricane, and the traditional brick structure is in rubble below the water.

The original tower stood seventy feet tall with a conical brick tower, eleven lamps and fourteen-inch reflectors. The first lighthouse keeper was to be Joseph Ximenez; however, the keeper at the Dry Tortugas Lighthouse, John Flaherty, and his wife, Rebecca, had trouble adjusting to a life of isolation. It was approved for keepers to switch assignments.

The couple enjoyed socializing with picnickers, fishermen and wreckers who came to Sand Key from Key West. Unfortunately, this joy ended when Flaherty fell ill in May 1828 and died in 1830. After his death, his wife remained on the island and was appointed the new Sand Key Lighthouse keeper.

Rebecca married Captain Fredrick Neill in November 1834, and after returning from their honeymoon, Neill was appointed the keeper of the lighthouse. He remained lighthouse keeper until February 10, 1836, when he retired from service. Several other lighthouse keepers came and went, as the assignment of watching the Sand Key Lighthouse was desirable to many keepers.

During the Havana Hurricane, Keeper Appleby's daughter, Eliza, visited the lighthouse with her three-year-old son; Mary Ann Petty Harris, a family friend; and Mary's adopted daughter. (More about Appleby is in the chapter about the Key West Lighthouse.) When the hurricane barreled through the Florida Keys, Appleby and the others hid in the lighthouse, believing it would withstand the storm in 1846 because it had held up to the many previous storms.

As the raging storm swept across the island, it washed away the lighthouse tower, the keeper's dwelling and the island. There was no trace of the lighthouse or those who sought refuge in the tower.

After the hurricane, the original lighthouse was replaced by a skeletal cast-iron pyramid in the hope the open metal structure would be more durable during storms and challenging open-water conditions. Luckily, this belief was proven valid, as this lighthouse has withstood high winds, hurricane storms and other open-water conditions.

Snorkeling is the most common activity around the Sand Key Lighthouse, and several visitors have reported seeing mysterious shadow figures hanging around the structure's cast-iron construction. It is unknown who these spirits belong to, but some feel they could be the spirits of boaters in the area during the Havana Hurricane who sought shelter in the brick lighthouse tower and lost their lives when the tower sank into the sea.

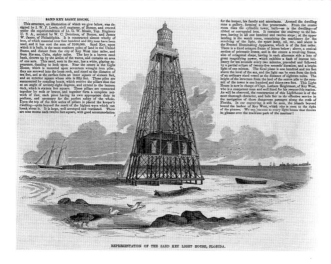

Representation of the Sand Key Lighthouse, Florida, S.E. Brown. *Library of Congress.*

Today the Sand Key Lighthouse's iron structure still stands over the dangerous reef below, but it was deactivated in 2014 by the Coast Guard because they determined the structure was unstable and unsafe. The historic structure is visited by snorkelers, many of whom are unaware of the lighthouse keepers, the island and the area's history. Who knows, maybe some of those who lost their lives in the Havana Hurricane quietly hide among the coral reef or go snorkeling side by side with the tourists.

Instead of Sand Key's lighthouse giving off the two flashes every fifteen seconds, it now illuminates from a nearby structure. After an auction, the Sand Key Lighthouse was sold to the highest bidder and is now privately owned.

22

CARYSFORT REEF LIGHT

KEY LARGO, FLORIDA

I can think of no other edifice constructed by man as altruistic as a lighthouse.
They were built only to serve.
—George Bernard Shaw

Nestled approximately six nautical miles east of Key Largo, the Carysfort Reef Light stands one hundred feet above the water. Before its decommissioning, it was the oldest functioning lighthouse of its kind in the United States. The light, which was constructed with an iron screw-pile foundation with a platform, was an octagonal pyramid design. Named for HMS *Carysfort* from 1766, the skeletal tower was decommissioned in 2015 and, in 1984, was added to the National Register of Historic Places.

In 1825, the original Carysfort Reef Light was built in New York City and named Caesar.[20] During transport to its destination, a storm rolled in, and the ship went aground, and the crew abandoned the vessel near Key Biscayne. After wreckers salvaged the ship, it was transported to Key West and placed on station at the Carysfort Reef; however, because of several intense storms in the area, the light was blown off-station several times and went aground on the reef. Due to damage and dry rot, it needed to be replaced within five years of the first light's placement.

In 1825, John Whalton was the captain of the Caesar Lightship and maintained his captainship when the first light was replaced. While he was captain, Seminoles burned the Cape Florida Lighthouse in 1836, leaving the Carysfort Reef Light the only navigational light between St. Augustine and

Key West. Later that same year, Captain Whalton and his helpers went ashore on Key Largo to tend to their garden at Garden Cove. Seminoles attacked the group, killing Captain Whalton and one of his helpers. The three others managed to escape back to the ship, with only two being wounded.

In the 1840s, Congress approved funds to construct a screw-pile lighthouse at Carysfort Reef. This lighthouse was the third of its kind in the country and was manufactured in Philadelphia, Pennsylvania, in 1848. However, the installation of the lighthouse was met with a series of troubles, including the discovery that the reef was not as solid as the government had expected. Plus, during the construction, the project supervisor died, and the U.S. Army Corps of Topographical Engineers appointed Lieutenant George Meade to oversee the remainder of the project. This lighthouse project was Meade's first command, and he later became the commander of the Army of the Potomac and victor at the Battle of Gettysburg.

After the Carysfort Reef Light was extinguished, it was announced on February 1, 2019, that it would be given away for free to any government agency, nonprofit corporation, educational agency or community development organization wanting to take over the property for educational, recreational and historical preservation projects. Then, according to the National Historic Lighthouse Preservation Act, if no one stepped up to manage the lighthouse for these purposes, it would be auctioned off to the highest bidder.

Along with two other lighthouses—Sombrero Key Lighthouse and American Shoal Lighthouse—the Carysfort Reef Light was put up for auction. On May 16, 2022,[21] the Carysfort Reef Light sold for a final bid of $415,000, the lowest amount among all three lighthouses sold during the same auction.

Today, the rusted-out lighthouse is something you would expect to see in a horror movie, and its ugliness is the perfect place for ghosts and unwanted supernatural beings to reside. Plus, the fact that this lighthouse is set among shark-infested waters adds to the spookiness for those who dare to take a boat out to the maritime beacon. Not to mention the dangerous waters, hidden reefs and unexpected sandbars make the journey to this lighthouse a unique experience for those who dare brave the seas and the supernatural entities.

Several legends claim the waters surrounding the Carysfort Reef Lighthouse are plagued with supernatural specters and creatures. For example, when the sun sets on the lighthouse, strange things happen; moans can be heard piercing the quiet night air, and the apparition of Captain

Whalton is believed to appear now and then before boaters who dare to brave the waters surrounding Carysfort Reef Lighthouse.

Sounds around the lighthouse and strange occurrences on the shores of Key Largo have paranormal researchers believing the activity could be tied to the Seminole ambush of Captain Whalton and his four assistants. Some think the moans and wails heard at night are from the captain's widow mourning the loss of her husband. Others claim the strange occurrences, shadow figures and noises on the shores of Key Largo are the energies of those involved in the Seminole attack, repeating their fate on the day they went ashore.

Another strange occurrence and story shared among many Florida paranormal research teams is that of a floating skeleton seen in the waters near the lighthouse at night, with a few pieces of clothing still attached to the legs and torso. Then, suddenly, the skeleton slowly fades away.

Other known hauntings at the Carysfort Reef Lighthouse include ghosts from past shipwrecks and the spirits of previous lighthouse keepers. Captain Alexander C. Jenks, the Carysfort Reef Lighthouse second assistant lighthouse keeper beginning around 1915 and keeper from 1927 to 1936, invited friends to stay the night at the lighthouse in the hopes they could prove the legends and rumors of ghosts were true. During this visit, one of his guests experienced humanlike groans, which were believed to belong to a former lighthouse captain. When the guest shared his story in the middle of the night with Captain Jenks, he replied that it was probably just "Old Captain Johnson" and nothing to worry about.[22]

Several visitors have heard strange creaking and groaning sounds when they are underneath the lighthouse; however, with the age of the Carysfort Reef Lighthouse, these noises could result from the deteriorated condition of the tower's structure. These structures are pulled back and forth with heavy water movements and waves, and they are subject to high winds and hurricane forces. The change in temperatures in the area can also cause the metal and steel framing to contract and expand as temperatures fluctuate.

Other visitors have reported hearing a whistling or howling sound when out by the lighthouse. The skeleton structure of the Carysfort Reef Lighthouse allows wind to blow through and, depending on the force of the wind and the direction it is coming from in relation to the lighthouse's position in the water, could cause the sounds some believe to be ghosts, demons or other supernatural entities.

Going back to the floating skeleton, some visitors have been startled by hearing an unexpected splash in the water behind them, and when they look, there is nothing there. A combination of hearing stories such as that of the skeleton or the spirits of pirates still haunting the waters could contribute to a person's mind playing games and causing them to think that they are surrounded by ghosts. In addition, the location of the Carysfort Reef Lighthouse is home to much marine wildlife, including fish and sharks, which may jump out of the water or make a splash as they approach the boat.

One more natural element contributing to the paranormal activity when visiting the waters below the Carysfort Reef Lighthouse could be dehydration. Depending on how long someone is out on the water in the hot Florida sun or scuba diving in the waters below, there is a slight risk they could become dehydrated. Dehydration can lead to tiredness and dizziness, which may add to a person's anxiousness about being surrounded by ghostly apparitions.

Is the Carysfort Lighthouse haunted? From the many reports of paranormal activity, it is definitely possible. But only once all possible natural occurrences and causes have been dismissed can this activity be determined paranormal. But as with any lighthouse in Florida, there is an excellent chance that former lightkeepers, pirates and others remain behind in the waters protecting the lighthouse, their loot or loved ones whom they feel may be left behind.

23

MOUNT DORA LIGHTHOUSE

MOUNT DORA, FLORIDA

Let hope be your lighthouse, beckoning you through stormy seas.
—Jessica de la Davies

W hen thinking about lighthouses, chances are many people only consider Florida lighthouses that are found along coastal regions with direct or close access to the Atlantic Ocean or the Gulf of Mexico. However, one lighthouse in Florida is set in the middle of the state and is often surprising to those who come upon the structure.

Mount Dora, Florida, is a charming town with antique stores, unique shops, quaint cafés and plenty of history to explore. This small town in Central Florida is home to beautiful parks, refreshing waterways and many things for residents and visitors to explore outdoors. One of the city's most popular attractions is Mount Dora Lighthouse, set on the shores of Lake Dora.

The small but mighty landmark is also known as the Grantham Point Lighthouse, and as it continues to stand in the quiet town, it has a fascinating story behind its creation and continued existence.

Unlike the other lighthouses in this book, the Mount Dora Lighthouse is slightly different. First, this lighthouse is not the gigantic towering lighthouses one expects to see on the coastal waters of Florida. Instead, the small but iconic lighthouse sits on the shores of Lake Dora, which is a series of interconnected lakes in Central Florida known as the Harris Chain of Lakes. The lakes and surrounding areas also have a unique history but are mostly known for the natural beauty surrounding these tranquil waterways.

In the 1800s, these lakes were frequently used by the first settlers to the area to transport goods and supplies to other towns along the waterways. The waterways continued to be used by fishermen and boaters through the decades and into the late 1900s.

Over time, fishermen and boaters found the waters of the Harris Chain of Lakes challenging to navigate and travel, especially from the town of Tavares to Mount Dora. When the sun sets, traveling these waterways is even more challenging than during the daytime. Because of the troubles fishermen and boaters faced at night, the idea of constructing a lighthouse in Mount Dora was born.

Travelers, locals and government officials in the area raised more than $3,000 to help design and construct the lighthouse, which stands only thirty-five feet in height. The Mount Dora Lighthouse officially started operation on March 25, 1988, and everyone was impressed by the brick base and stucco surface painted in beautiful red and white stripes.

The most iconic thing about the lighthouse is that it is the only inland freshwater lighthouse in the entire state of Florida. The second most iconic thing about Mount Dora are the many spirits who call this quaint small town home in the afterlife.

Many spirits reported in Mount Dora are found walking the streets of downtown or in one of the many buildings, including the Lakeside Inn and the Donnelly House.

Some people who have visited the lighthouse at night have heard strange sounds, but many believe they are the sounds from the animals living in and around Lake Dora's waters. Others have witnessed strange shadows, glimpses of apparitions and bright light anomalies flashing over the waters.

The paranormal activity near the Mount Dora Lighthouse could be related to the many paranormal reports within the town. Still, it could also be associated with the history of boaters and fishermen who had trouble navigating the waters at night. This area of Central Florida requires more investigation to be sure of what is happening and to hopefully capture evidence of ghostly apparitions hanging out near the Mount Dora Lighthouse.

24

JOHN'S PASS FAUX LIGHTHOUSE

MADEIRA BEACH, FLORIDA

A smooth sea never made a skilled sailor.
—Franklin D. Roosevelt

The quote from Franklin D. Roosevelt holds true for a pirate, too, and the Madeira Beach area is no stranger to pirate activity, which makes this quote perfect for this chapter. John's Pass Village is a small fishing village in Madeira Beach close to St. Petersburg and home to many unique shops, fabulous restaurants and plenty of opportunities to enjoy time on the water.

One of the most iconic features of John's Pass Village is the faux lighthouse that sits near Hubbard's Marina and Hooters Restaurant. This faux lighthouse is the centerpiece of the shopping area, complete with a boardwalk and several shops featuring unique pirate-themed goodies available for purchase.

The decorative lighthouse sits inside the pass, which leads into the Gulf of Mexico and can be spotted from the waters surrounding the local marinas.

Those enjoying the hustle and bustle of the John's Pass Village may not notice they are not alone as they walk the boardwalk and enjoy the many elements of this idyllic fishing village on Florida's west coast. Those enjoying the beautiful place by eating on an outdoor patio, taking a guided dolphin cruise or exploring the local area know about the spirits that remain behind in Madeira Beach; they may never look at the location the same again.

Above: Faux Lighthouse at John's Pass in Madeira Beach, Florida. *Heather Leigh, PhD.*

Opposite: Faux Lighthouse at John's Pass in Madeira Beach, Florida. *Heather Leigh, PhD.*

The areas around the lighthouse and throughout John's Pass Village are littered with paranormal activity. Those who know where and what to look for may be lucky enough to see something spooky and even supernatural in nature.

Formerly located in the area was the notorious Shanty Hogan Saloon, which was a place for nefarious activity with a shady reputation. The saloon fell victim to a fire, which destroyed the house of ill repute that once existed upstairs from the saloon. Today, Delosa's Pizza is in the location where the Shanty Hogan Saloon once stood. Visitors and employees at the famous pizza joint claim to hear footsteps pacing back and forth upstairs when no second floor exists. The sounds of a "stomp-click" similar to that belonging to a peg-legged man are also reported coming from the ghostly upstairs.

Though it closed down in the 1970s, across the way from the faux John's Pass Lighthouse was the Marine Arena, where performing dolphins Patty (or Paddy) and Mike, named after the Hubbard siblings, and Frank, were a main attraction for those visiting the Madeira Beach and Treasure Island areas. Unfortunately, a storm struck the area and created a way for Frank and Mike to escape, leaving poor Patty behind to mourn the loss of the companionship he grew to love and depend upon.

Patty was discovered dead in his tank in November 1967, and eventually, the Arena ceased operations. After the Arena officially closed, those who passed by the shuttered structure could hear the echoing squeals of Patty crying out for his lost mates from the abandoned facility.

Another chilling tale arising from Madeira Beach is that of two brothers who were farmers in the area and were believed to be Union sympathizers during the Civil War. These brothers were set up by Confederate guerrillas at John's Pass while bringing in supplies from Egmont Key. The brothers were brutally attacked, and one of the brothers sustained life-threatening injuries.

Fishermen heading out in the predawn hours following a new moon have reported seeing two emaciated figures cross John's Pass in a skiff. As the fishermen get closer to the skiff, they are met with an overwhelming scent of decaying flesh. This story has had many variations, including seeing the two brothers dressed in Confederate uniforms walking over the John's Pass Bridge and disappearing as the living approach them or as they reach the top of the bridge's cap.

Additionally, the spirit of Wilson Hubbard, the patriarch of Hubbard's Marina, who passed away in 1994, remains behind and watches over the marina's operations.

Other reports of paranormal activity around the John's Pass Village include the sensation of someone standing behind a person, and then, when they turn around, no one is there. Some visitors have claimed to see a person standing behind them as they look in the window of various shops and restaurants on the boardwalk, and when they turn around, no one is directly behind them. Apparitions have been spotted on the sandy beach on the far east side of the boardwalk, and then, on closer look, the spirit vanishes into thin air.

Is it safe to say that the area around the John's Pass Village faux lighthouse is haunted? Of course, it is. These are just some of the many stories passed around among employees, fishermen, boaters, tour guides, residents and visitors of the area.

When exploring John's Pass Village, it is not an uncommon occurrence to feel a ghostly apparition following a person around or see a shadow figure dart across the field of vision from the corner of the eye. As with the real lighthouses in Florida, the faux lighthouse in Madeira Beach, Florida, acts as a beacon attracting paranormal activity to thrive in the area of John's Pass Village.

25

SULFUR SPRINGS WATER TOWER

TAMPA BAY, FLORIDA

Third eye of the sea, the lonely lighthouse never sleeps.
—Nanette L. Avery

The Tampa Bay area in Southwest Florida is full of pockets of historical significance scattered throughout the region where visitors can experience what life was like during the state's early days. In addition, many sites throughout the area are filled with mystery and plagued with strange occurrences believed to be paranormal activity.

One intriguing site in Tampa Bay is a few miles north of downtown in historic Sulphur Springs, a quiet neighborhood where locals and travelers would enjoy relaxing at its serene mineral springs back in the late 1800s. Today, Sulphur Springs is home to a tall water tower, which has become a historic landmark; it replaced another landmark important to the area's development.

The 214-foot-tall water tower is an impressive sight and can be seen high above swaying palm trees near Florida's Interstate 275. Anywhere in Sulphur Springs one can see the magnificent white water tower that constantly reminds residents of the area's historic and tragic past.

Many moons ago, a lighthouse stood where the Sulphur Springs Water Tower stands today. The lighthouse protected the area's shores as it stood to watch against invaders and pirates while guiding ship captains needing assistance navigating along the Tampa Bay section of the Gulf coastline. After years of dedicated service, the lighthouse was demolished, leaving a dark void in its absence until the water tower was erected.

In the 1920s, many years after the lighthouse was demolished, Sulphur Springs was believed to be a great area to make a tourist attraction and attract people worldwide. Josiah Richardson knew about the area's reputation for having healing waters. He used this to his advantage, and in an effort to attract more visitors, he started construction on the Sulphur Springs Hotel and Apartments, followed by the opening of Mave's Arcade, Florida's first indoor shopping venue, on the building's first floor.

Richardson had big dreams and enormous ambitions, and the building he planned to build, nestled on the corner of Bird Street and Nebraska Avenue, was intended to have a luxurious spa retreat. But to attract visitors interested in learning more about Florida's culture and wildlife, he also planned to have an alligator farm nearby for tours and for visitors to see these horribly fierce creatures up close and personal.

Over time, Richardson discovered there was not enough water pressure for his attractions, and he needed to develop a solution for his problems. Desperate, he was forced to mortgage the Sulphur Springs Hotel and Apartments to collect enough money to fund the construction of the 200,000-gallon water tower constructed by Grover Pool. The massive water tower was a huge investment and would only add to the value and desirability of visiting Richardson's resort area. Unfortunately, even though the water tower's construction was advancing daily, Richardson's idea of creating a popular tourist attraction was short-lived.

The resort Richardson worked so hard to develop and promote was rushed by water in 1933 when the Tampa Electric Company's dam was intentionally destroyed. Unfortunately, Mave's Arcade and the Sulphur Springs Hotel and Apartments were so severely damaged that all the shops inside the arcade were abruptly closed. After putting his heart, soul and finances into the development of the Sulphur Springs Hotels and Apartments, Richardson saw his heavily mortgaged investment destroyed before his eyes and eventually found himself bankrupt.

Property development in the Sulphur Springs area came to a halt as tourist activity nearly stopped during the Great Depression, and this once-bustling area in Tampa Bay was now eerily quiet and resembled a ghost town.

Unfortunately, in September 1929, when the stock market plummeted and started a years-long depression, many families and businesspeople were left in despair and dire economic situations. There was not one person immune to the Great Depression, as unemployment rates skyrocketed and even those among the wealthiest in the country lost their livelihood.

As sadness and desperation spread through the Tampa Bay area, many residents who believed they had nowhere else to turn sought refuge in the Sulfur Springs Water Tower to end what they thought to be eternal suffering. Unfortunately, many residents affected by the Great Depression had frantic reactions and made rash decisions that affected their lives and the lives of their loved ones.

Many people believed there was only one way to escape the feeling of hopelessness caused by the financial strain on the economy and turned to suicide as a means to stop their pain and suffering. It is believed that at least forty thousand Americans took their lives in the years of the Great Depression due to the events that followed the financial collapse of the country's economy. Several desperate Floridians made their way to the Sulphur Springs Water Tower to use it as an opportunity to escape their lives and what was believed to be an unavoidable fate.

The Tower Theater, a drive-in movie theater, opened and brought new life to the area in 1951. This theater became a popular place where locals and visitors would hang out and enjoy the latest movies under the shadow of the Sulphur Springs Water Tower. The Tower Theater was easily identifiable, especially after erecting the neon tower, mimicking the original water tower. The drive-in movie theater would remain a popular entertainment destination for those wanting to watch the latest films for the next forty years.

In the end, after all the dreams and attempts to make Sulphur Springs a tourist and entertainment destination, a residential complex was proposed to be considered for development around the base of the water tower. However, this dream did not become a reality either, and the property would remain empty until it was transformed into a beautiful park.

In 1989, the Sulphur Springs Water Tower underwent extensive clean-up and renovation. First, the tower's surface was power washed, freeing the structure of years of debris; then Sherwin Williams enlisted the help of others to lead a massive painting project. The company donated more than 150 gallons of graffiti-proof white paint that were applied to the water tower, giving it a new life.

In 2005, the City of Tampa purchased the tower and installed lighting to help illuminate the area, which still has a small park surrounding the tower's base. Unfortunately, however, this park has no desirable amenities and often sits quietly, with no visitors or activity expected of a southwestern Florida park.

Though there is little information about the lighthouse at Sulfur Springs, it is interesting that the land it once stood on and watched over is now home to many spirits. Some spirits could be the remnants of the old lighthouse days, while many others are believed to belong to those who leaped to their death during the Great Depression and other tragic events in the community.

Though these people believed that this was their only way to be relieved of their pain and a means to exit their current path, several have stayed behind and haunted the grounds surrounding the water tower. Because of the land's past, it is not surprising that the Sulfur Springs Water Tower is a location for many spectral sightings, a few eerie occurrences and tons of unexplained phenomena. Many who have visited or investigated the area just underneath and around the water tower have returned home as witnesses to supernatural events and have unique and mysterious tales to tell.

One ghostly tale coming from Sulfur Springs is that of a man dressed in Depression-era clothing seen pacing back and forth at the top of the tower. As he slowly walks, witnesses say they can see he is clearly contemplating his fate and is still burdened with the sadness and despair he was suffering when living.

Another chilling tale is that of a woman apparition also spotted at the top of the tower. Her tortured spirit is often seen pacing around the top of the tower, and then she abruptly plunges toward the ground below. However, the plummet to her death is not completed, as she does not hit the ground, and her apparition is said to disappear moments before impact.

This female spirit is not the only spirit that has been spotted jumping off the tower to the ground below. Those who witness these spirits reliving their final moments are left to wonder if the spirits are unsettled about the method they chose to end their lives or if they have been doomed to live eternity trying to gain an understanding of their sadness experienced during the Great Depression.

Other spirits that haunt the grounds of the Sulphur Springs Water Tower are those believed to be attached to the energy left behind by the former lighthouse. Because of the lighthouse's unique connection with the sea, it is thought that many pirate ghosts make their presence known to those near the current water tower.

One Sulphur Springs legend is that the lighthouse served as a marker used on an infamous treasure map and pirates relied on it, believing it would guide them to their loot when ready. Unfortunately for the pirates, when the lighthouse was destroyed, they lost their treasured landmark that was the guiding light to their buried riches.

Apparitions dressed in pirate gear have been spotted walking and searching around the water tower's base, searching for any clues to lead them to the hidden treasure. Some witnesses have also claimed to see a ghost pirate ship sailing the Hillsborough River with no decisive explanation for its movement, and it drifts toward what is believed to be the final spot on their quest. The pirates spotted are likely to be the unsettled pirates who continue to wander the Earth looking to recover the treasure they lost during the unfortunate interruption to their mission when the lighthouse was destroyed.

The Sulphur Springs Water Tower and the former location of a lighthouse are home to many apparitions. Those who visit the park, go boating along the Hillsborough River or drive along Highway 275 may be lucky enough to catch a glimpse of an apparition or a ghost ship. One thing is for sure. When exploring this area of Tampa, it is vital to keep an open mind and be ready to encounter anything supernatural.

Author's Notes

I first want to thank you for reading *Haunted Florida Lighthouses*. I hope you enjoyed reading it as much as I enjoyed writing it. Researching and investigating these areas took many years, and watching it all come together was like watching your child grow into adulthood.

Living in Florida for many years, seeing magnificent lighthouses along the shoreline and exploring the communities that house these beautiful structures provided the inspiration to continue researching and learning more about the history behind the many paranormal rumors and urban legends related to some of Florida's many lighthouses.

Ultimately, my goal for this book is to help those wanting to learn more about Florida's history associated with lighthouses and the many legends passed down through the generations in these areas. Additionally, I wanted to share how the history of the Sunshine State's lighthouses affects the paranormal activity witnessed throughout the state. Finally, I hope the book provides information for those seeking to travel throughout Florida looking to see the many fabulous lighthouses and those wanting to see the darker side of the state while coming face to face with the spirits that live around these lighthouses.

My writing process for this book differed from other books I have done in the past, mainly because a lot of the work was completed many years ago when I visited and investigated these locations. To help finish the book, I contacted fellow paranormal researchers to see if there had been any new reports or updates regarding paranormal activity near Florida's lighthouse.

Plus, the fact that I had knee replacement surgery during the writing process did delay things a bit longer than I anticipated. But in the end, I feel this has been a fantastic adventure and worth the wait.

Speaking with fellow researchers and investigators was one of my favorite parts of writing this book. I have always loved hearing the stories and experiences of others and was amazed at how many stories at Florida's lighthouses were similar from researcher to researcher. In most of my other research, though there are parallel accounts of paranormal activity, there is typically a wide range of activity, entities encountered and related experiences. That said, most of the lighthouse spirits in Florida may be residual, and the ones that make their appearance known are not afraid of the living visiting.

After more than thirty years of researching and investigating the paranormal, I want to share what I have learned with others. More paranormal encounters, legends, stories and personal experiences are featured in my first two books with The History Press: *Haunted Southern Nevada Ghost Towns* and *Ghosts and Legends of the Vegas Valley*.

Thank you again for reading *Haunted Florida Lighthouses*, and I look forward to bringing you more amazing paranormal stories and encounters throughout Florida.

NOTES

1. "Meloria Tower," Atlas Obscura, https://www.atlasobscura.com.
2. "Florida Lighthouses," Florida Lighthouses, https://floridalighthouses.org.
3. "Florida's Historic Lighthouses," Exploring Florida, https://fcit.usf.edu.
4. "Home," St. Augustine Lighthouse, https://www.staugustinelighthouse.org.
5. "St. Augustine Lighthouse," US Ghost Adventures, https://usghostadventures.com.
6. "Saint Augustine Lighthouse," Haunted Houses, http://hauntedhouses.com.
7. "Port Boca Grande (Gasparilla Island) Lighthouse," LighthouseFriends, https://www.lighthousefriends.com.
8. "Pensacola Lighthouse Considered One of Most Haunted in America." WKRG News 5, October 31, 2019, https://www.wkrg.com.
9. "Florida Lighthouses—Ponce de Leon Lighthouse," Ponce Inlet Lighthouse and Museum, www.ponceinlet.org.
10. St. George Island Lighthouse Museum & Gift Shop on St. George Island Florida, https://www.stgeorgelight.org/.
11. "Terrifying Witch Seeks Revenge on Predators at This Florida State Park," Backpackerverse, February 21, 2017. https://backpackerverse.com.
12. "Hillsboro Inlet Lighthouse," LighthouseFriends, https://www.lighthousefriends.com.
13. "Cape San Blas Lighthouse," LighthouseFriends, https://www.lighthousefriends.com.
14. Toni Collins, "Cedar Key News: Seahorse Key's Haunting History," Cedar Keys News, https://cedarkeynews.com.

15. "Cedar Keys (Seahorse Key) Lighthouse," LighthouseFriends, https://www.lighthousefriends.com.
16. Crooked River Lighthouse, www.crookedriverlighthouse.com.
17. "Sanibel Island Lighthouse," LighthouseFriends, https://www.lighthousefriends.com.
18. "Amelia Island Lighthouse," Fernandina Beach, http://fbfl.us.
19. "Mayport: Old St. Johns Lighthouse," Jax Psycho Geo, June 21, 2012, https://jaxpsychogeo.com.
20. "Carysfort Reef Lighthouse," Southern Most Ghosts, October 23, 2020, https://southernmostghosts.com.
21. Alex Rickert, "Auctions Close for 3 Iconic Keys Lighthouses," Florida Keys Weekly Newspapers, May 27, 2022, https://keysweekly.com.
22. "The Carysfort Lighthouse Ghost," Island Jane, September 1, 2017, http://islandjanemagazine.com.

BIBLIOGRAPHY

Abraham Lincoln's Assassination. "The Text of George Atzerodt's Lost Confession." https://rogerjnorton.com.

Amelia Island Florida. "Hauntingly Good Times on Amelia Island and Beyond." September 14, 2022. https://www.ameliaisland.com.

Ayers, Wayne. "John's Pass Ghosts Unearthed." TBNweekly, February 21, 2005. https://www.tbnweekly.com.

bubs. "Headless Pirate of Seahorse Key." Haunted Places. https://www.hauntedplaces.org.

Cipra, David L. *Lighthouses, Lightships, and the Gulf of Mexico*. Alexandria, VA: Cypress Communications, 1997.

D'Entremont, Jemery. "Sanibel Lighthouse: A Constant through Storm and Change." *Lighthouse Digest*, July 2001.

Dr. Samuel A. Mudd House Museum. "Dr. Samuel A. Mudd House Museum." https://drmudd.org.

Florida Lighthouse Association. "Florida Lighthouses." https://floridalighthouses.org.

Florida State Parks. "Port Boca Grande Lighthouse and Museum | Florida State Parks." www.floridastateparks.org.

Florida's Forgotten Coast. "St George Island Lighthouse—Carrabelle Lighthouse." https://www.floridasforgottencoast.com.

Ghost City Tours. "The 1846 Key West Hurricane." https://ghostcitytours.com.

Ghosts and Gravestones. "Key West Ghost Tours | Key West Haunted Tours." https://www.ghostsandgravestones.com.

———. "St. Augustine Lighthouse Haunted Guide." https://www.ghostsandgravestones.com.

Haunted Places. "Ponce de Leon Inlet Lighthouse." https://www.hauntedplaces.org.

Homestead, Mailing Address: 40001 SR-9336, and FL 33034 Phone: 305 242-7700 Contact Us. "Lighthouses—Dry Tortugas National Park (U.S. National Park Service)." National Park Service. https://www.nps.gov.

Jenkins, Greg. 2007. *Florida's Ghostly Legends and Haunted Folklore: The Gulf Coast and Pensacola*. Sarasota, FL: Pineapple Press, 2007.

Jupiter Inlet Lighthouse and Museum. "Home." https://www.jupiterlighthouse.org/.

Mysterious Universe. "The Bizarre Case of the St. Johns River Monster." mysteriousuniverse.org.

National Park Service. "Dry Tortugas National Park (U.S. National Park Service)." https://www.nps.gov.

Nightly Spirits. "The Sulphur Springs Water Tower—Haunted Tampa—Nightly Spirits." https://nightlyspirits.com.

Nipps, Emily. "Explore the Cape Florida Lighthouse at Key Biscayne in Miami." Visit Florida, July 25, 2017. https://www.visitflorida.com.

Pensacola Lighthouse and Maritime Museum. "Pensacola Lighthouse." https://www.pensacolalighthouse.org/.

Roman, Marisa. "The Iconic Mount Dora Lighthouse in Florida Is Small but Mighty." Only In Your State, April 7, 2022. https://www.onlyinyourstate.com.

Southern Most Ghosts. "Carysfort Reef Lighthouse." October 23, 2020, https://southernmostghosts.com.

———. "Fort Jefferson in the Dry Tortugas." September 24, 2020, https://southernmostghosts.com.

———. "The Key West Light House." November 2, 2019, https://southernmostghosts.com.

Tuscaloosa Paranormal Research Group. "Pensacola Lighthouse." https://tuscaloosaparanormal.com.

U.S. Lighthouses. "St. John's River Lighthouse." https://us-lighthouses.com.

ABOUT THE AUTHOR

Heather Leigh Carroll-Landon, PhD, started her journey in the paranormal field as a teenager after multiple interactions with her grandfather, who passed away many years before. She has researched and traveled to locations to learn more about the history of the land, buildings and local area and paranormal claims. As long as she has been interested in the supernatural, Heather Leigh has been a freelance writer, writing for several newspapers, magazines and online publications. She and her family (Exploration Paranormal) appeared in *Real Haunts: Ghost Towns* and *Real Haunts 3*, where they explored many southern Nevada ghost towns.

She is an author of articles and books and a lecturer about all things paranormal. Her first book, *Haunted Southern Nevada Ghost Towns*, was published by The History Press in August 2022, and her second book, *Ghosts and Legends of the Vegas Valley*, was also published by The History Press in February 2023. She has many more book ideas in the works and hopes to bring them to life in the near future.

She holds a Doctor of Philosophy degree in Metaphysical and Humanistic Science with a specialty in Paranormal Science. She is a Certified Paranormal Investigator and a Certified EVP Technician. She aims to help others take a more scientific approach to paranormal investigations and research.

Heather Leigh is a co-host and content contributor for *Touch of Magick*, a podcast about magick and the supernatural. Heather Leigh is also the founder of Exploration Paranormal and host of *Exploring the Paranormal* and co-host of *Passport to the Paranormal* with Joe Franke *on* WLTK-DB Radio. She also co-hosts *Ghost Education 101* vodcasts with Philip R. Wyatt on Facebook and YouTube. You can find Heather Leigh on Facebook (@DrHeatherLeigh), where you will find additional information, including upcoming classes, lectures and more, or via her websites, www.heatherleighphd.com and www.explorationparanormal.com.

FREE eBOOK OFFER

Scan the QR code below, enter your e-mail address and get our original Haunted America compilation eBook delivered straight to your inbox for free.

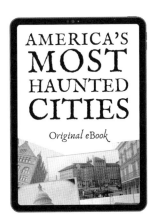

ABOUT THE BOOK

Every city, town, parish, community and school has their own paranormal history. Whether they are spirits caught in the Bardo, ancestors checking on their descendants, restless souls sending a message or simply spectral troublemakers, ghosts have been part of the human tradition from the beginning of time.

In this book, we feature a collection of stories from five of America's most haunted cities: Baltimore, Chicago, Galveston, New Orleans and Washington, D.C.

SCAN TO GET
AMERICA'S MOST HAUNTED CITIES

Having trouble scanning? Go to:
biz.arcadiapublishing.com/americas-most-haunted-cities

Visit us at
www.historypress.com